How do I survive?

Index

abomination: 26°c, 24°c, 22°c
agriculture: 27°c, 25°c, 22°c
afterlife: 24°c, 21°c
aliens: 28°c
      alien love: 23°c
      alien worlds: 28°c
Allende, Salvador: 26°c
anachronism: 20°c
anarchy: 30°c
ancestors: 28°c, 26°c
angels: 20°c
      deranged angels: 29°c
animality: 25°c, 23°c, 19°c, 18°c
      animal instincts: 26°c
Antarctica: 22°c
art: 31°c, 17°c, 16°c
      living museum: 22°c
      sculpture: 20°c
      self-referential: 16°c
atmosphere: 33°c, 29°c, 21°c
      clouds: 32°c
dust and gas: 31°c, 22°c
nitrogen surfaces: 22°c
warming: 27°c
biology: 28°c, 21°c, 20°c
      biological age: 31°c
      biotechnology company: 28°c
      biologically transient: 21°c
      biologist: 28°c
      laboratory: 29°c

lab rat: 24°c
blood: 25°c
        blood-sucking: 23°c
        lifeblood: 26°c
        vessels: 25°c, 24°c
boredom: 26°c
bowels: 19°c
brain: 30°c, 28°c, 26°c, 25°c, 18°c
        collective brain: 26°c
brain adaption: 31°c, 30°c, 28°c, 22°c
pineal gland: 20°c
Brazil: 22°c
California: 29°c, 24°c
cancer: 20°c
carbon: 33°c, 22°c, 21°c
        atmospheric: 33°c
        lifecycle: 22°c
        retention-cycle: 22°c
        sequestration: 22°c
        sink: 22°c
Carpenter, John: 23°c
charity: 20°c
chemical manufacturing: 31°c
Chevron: 17°c
children: 33°c, 26°c, 24°c, 23°c, 22°c
        childhood: 26°c
        childish: 20°c
China: 25°c ,22°c
claustrophile: 24°c
climate change: 33°c, 28°c, 27°c
        adaptation: 27°c
clocks: 28°c, 24°c
colonies: 29°c, 25°c

communism: 30°c
complicity: 26°c
concrete: 28°c, 27°c, 24°c
Connecticut River: 29°c
conspiracy: 26°c, 22°c, 20°c, 17°c
consciousness: 31°c, 28°c, 22°c, 21°c, 19°c, 18°c
        collective unconscious: 24°c
        development of: 31°c
        holographic: 28°c
        self-consciousness: 27°c, 17°c
contagion: 25°c
coping: 32°c, 27°c, 28°c, 21°c, 20°c, 18°c
cosmos: 33°c, 31°c, 29°c, 28°c, 20°c, 18°c, 17°c
        gas giant: 25°c
        nova: 29°c
        universe: 31°c, 29°c, 28°c, 19°c, 17°c
Dark Incantations: 28°c
death: 31°c, 30°c, 27°c, 26°c, 24°c, 23°c, 21°c, 18°c, 17°c
        corpse: 26°c, 20°c
        dead animals: 23°c
        the cure for death: 23°c
        the dead: 30°c, 28°c, 24°c, 22°c, 21°c, 20°c, 18°c
        skulls: 19°c
deities: 22°c, 17°c
demons: 25°c, 22°c, 17°c
Divine glow: 18°c
democracy: 22°c
denial: 19°c, 17°c
desert: 26°c, 25°c, 22°c, 20°c
        desert world: 22°c, 21°c
desire: 32°c, 30°c, 29°c, 27°c, 23°c, 18°c, 17°c
        energetic: 30°c
        unconscious: 26°c

dependency: 30°c, 27°c, 26°c, 20°c
     mutualism: 30°c, 21°c
disaster: 33°c, 30°c, 27°c, 19°c
disease: 33°c, 26°c
     delusional disease: 18°c
dreams: 31°c, 29°c, 26°c, 23°c, 22°c, 21°c, 20°c, 19°c
     nightmares: 25°c, 17°c
drought: 28°c
dualism: 32°c
Earth: 26°c, 22°c
eBay: 23°c
economic growth: 21°c
     slush funds: 29°c
economic theory: 26°c
     clean energy economy: 22°c
     demand-side analysis: 29°c
     free market: 26°c
Economist, The: 20°c
eggs: 25°c, 23°c
embryo: 28°c
empire: 27°c, 20°c
engineering:
     engineer: 30°c, 28°c, 23°c
Enron: 17°c
environmental renewal: 19°c
evolution: 33°c, 21°c
     macro-evolutionary phase: 33°c
exhibitionism: 22°c, 21°c, 20°c
exoskeleton: 18°c
extinction: 30°c, 27°c, 23°c
     Extinction Age: 17°c
fertilizers: 29°c
fiber-optics: 24°c

film: 23°c, 21°c
food: 32°c, 30°c, 27°c, 25°c, 22°c, 21°c, 18°c
        Food Bank: 25°c
        food processor: 25°c
folklore: 29°c
frustration: 20°c, 17°c
        economic: 26°c
geological epoch: 33°c
germs: 31°c, 29°c
ghosts: 23°c, 21°c
globalization: 28°c
glyph: 18°c
God: 31°c, 23°c, 21°c, 20°c
        acts of: 30°c
government: 29°c
        Ministry for the Environment: 22°c
        Office of the Peoples' Government: 29°c
grimoire: 21°c
hallucinogen: 24°c
happiness: 32°c, 30°c, 28°c, 26°c, 23°c
heaven: 30°c, 24°c, 22°c
heat, conveniences of: 30°c
Hell:
        personal hell: 23°c
hibernation: 23°c
homeostasis: 19°c
        homeostats: 21°c
Honeywell: 17°c
hospitals: 20°c
hunger: 32°c, 30°c, 27°c, 26°c, 25°c
        famine: 32°c, 23°c
ignorance: 30°c, 29°c, 28°c, 24°c
immortality: 30°c, 22°c

industry: 30°c, 29°c, 22°c
        capitalist mode of production: 32°c
        chemical manufacturing: 31°c
        factory: 30°c, 29°c
        industrial age: 30°c
        small businesses: 29°c
information: 30°c, 22°c
        density of: 20°c
        information overload: 20°c
        storage: 23°c
intelligence: 17°c
        artificial: 30°c
        intelligence gathering: 20°c
        pure intelligence: 30°c
self-intelligence: 24°c
intellectual property: 19°c
interspecies competition: 20°c
interstellar matter: 27°c
Ireland: 29°c
job precarity: 26°c, 25°c
Kennebec National Laboratory: 24°c
Kropotkin, Peter: 23°c
library: 23°c
lifespan:
        carbon: 22°c
        human: 22°c
love: 29°c, 27°c, 25°c, 24°c, 23°c, 20°c
        intergenerational: 20°c
        unconditional: 23°c
Lessening: 30°c
machine: 31°c, 30°c, 29°c, 28°c, 26°c, 25°c, 23°c, 22°c, 21°c, 19°c
        biological: 33°c, 22°c, 18°c
        cyborg past: 29°c

floating: 21°c
invented by chance: 28°c
superfluous: 19°c
        virtual: 22°c
mammals: 23°c, 22°c
Mars: 21°c
        Martian: 21°c
        Red Planet: 21°c
memory: 28°c, 27°c, 26°c, 16°c
        computer-memory: 23°c
        memory loss: 28°c
metabolism: 25°c, 21°c
metals: 31°c, 29°c, 27°c, 24°c, 22°c, 21°c
Middle Ages: 22°c
migration: 29°c, 26°c, 25°c, 22°c
Ministry for the Environment: 22°c
mirrors: 29°c, 20°c
models: 33°c
        cognitive model: 20°c
        evolutionary: 17°c
        mind-map: 20°c
        planetary: 21°c
        wooden: 24°c
modernity: 30°c, 28°c, 20°c
        postmodernity: 17°c
monopolies: 26°c
mountains: 28°c, 26°c, 21°c, 19°c
        North Pacific: 21°c
        of carbon: 21°c
        of content: 30°c
Mount Philippine Beach: 29°c
mutuality: 30°c, 29°c
natural selection: 26°c

neuroscience: 31°c, 30°c
non-human: 26°c, 23°c, 21°c
objectification: 25°c, 22°c
ocean: 33°c, 30°c, 27°c, 22°c, 21°c, 17°c
        seafloor: 19°c
        Pacific: 29°c
occultism: 26°c, 21°c
        biomancy: 27°c
Office of the Peoples' Government: 29°c
oligarchy: 23°c
        land owners: 28°c
Paine, Thomas: 17°c
painkillers: 23°c
paranoia: 27°c
parasitism: 31°c, 29°c, 25°c, 18°c
parents: 28°c, 26°c, 25°c, 23°c, 21°c, 19°c
Paris: 29°c
peasants: 27°c
petroleum: 27°c, 25°c, 22°c
        fossil fuel industry: 30°c, 17°c
        petro-synthesis: 20°c
photosynthesis: 27°c
planet: 33°c, 25°c, 22°c, 21°c, 19°c, 18°c, 17°c, 16°c
        artificial: 19°c
        moon: 22°c
        planet-eating: 20°c
        planetary-self: 20°c
        planet-state: 20°c
        second Earth: 22°c
plutocrats: 27°c
politicians: 22°c
        children of: 22°c
postmodernity: 17°c

primates: 29°c, 26°c
prophecy: 32°c, 30°c, 29°c, 26°c
        crystal balls: 29°c, 26°c
        foresight syndrome: 20°c
omen: 29°c
        prophets: 29°c
prosthetics: 25°c, 21°c
psychology: 33°c, 32°c, 30°c
        social components of personality: 32°c
radiation: 25°c
rain: 25°c
redemption: 18°c
redemptive rains: 25°c
renewable energy: 22°c
resilience: 27°c, 26°c, 23°c
resurrection: 30°c
revolution:
global: 21°c
land grab: 25°c
nineteenth century: 21°c
rivers: 28°c
Romanticism: 32°c
sacrifice: 27°c, 23°c, 18°c
scarcity: 25°c, 18°c
scapegoating: 18°c
scavenging: 25°c, 22°c
science: 32°c, 30°c, 29°c, 28°c, 21°c
discoveries: 28°c
methods: 30°c
scientists: 33°c, 27°c, 23°c
scientific inquiry: 21°c
security: 30°c, 26°c, 22°c
seeds: 27°c

self-containment program: 16°c
self-sufficiency: 27°c, 24°c
sex: 26°c, 25°c
Silicon Beach: 25°c
silence: 29°c, 28°c
sin: 29°c
social movements:
        post-Katrina social change: 29°c
        Students of the Order Movement: 29°c
solar system: 29°c, 23°c, 21°c, 20°c
Soviet Union: 20°c
Space Age: 20°c
space travel: 22°c, 21°c, 20°c
squatting: 29°c
stars: 32°c, 29°c, 25°c, 21°c
status quo: 25°c
strangers: 29°c
stress: 27°c, 21°c
sun: 27°c, 23°c, 20°c, 19°c
symbiosis: 18°c
systems: 31°c, 26°c, 21°c
        capitalist: 32°c, 21°c
closed: 21°c
digestive: 19°c
        imaginary: 19°c
nervous: 19°c, 17°c
planetary: 21°c
        system of images: 19°c
        techno-social: 21°c
technology companies: 28°c, 21°c
telepathic tape: 19°c
transcendence: 29°c, 27°c
unemployment: 26°c, 25°c, 21°c

United States of America: 22°c, 20°c
utopia: 26°c
urbanism: 26°c, 25°c, 22°c
vanity project: 18°c
Venn diagram: 19°c
Victorian learning: 28°c
vitamins: 20°c
war: 28°c, 27°c, 26°c
civil: 27°c, 26°c
cold-war: 27°c, 20°c
Common Industrial War: 26°c
game of elimination: 21°c
of attrition: 19°c
waste: 33°c, 32°c, 25°c, 23°c, 22°c, 18°c
        energetic: 33°c
        feces: 24°c, 22°c, 17°c
        human trash: 22°c
        molecular: 29°c
waste people: 31°c, 23°c
water: 30°c, 25°c, 22°c, 21°c
wealth: 28°c, 24°c
        well-off families: 23°c
wood: 20°c, 24°c
workers: 29°c, 26°c, 25°c
working class: 21°c
wound: 25°c, 17°c

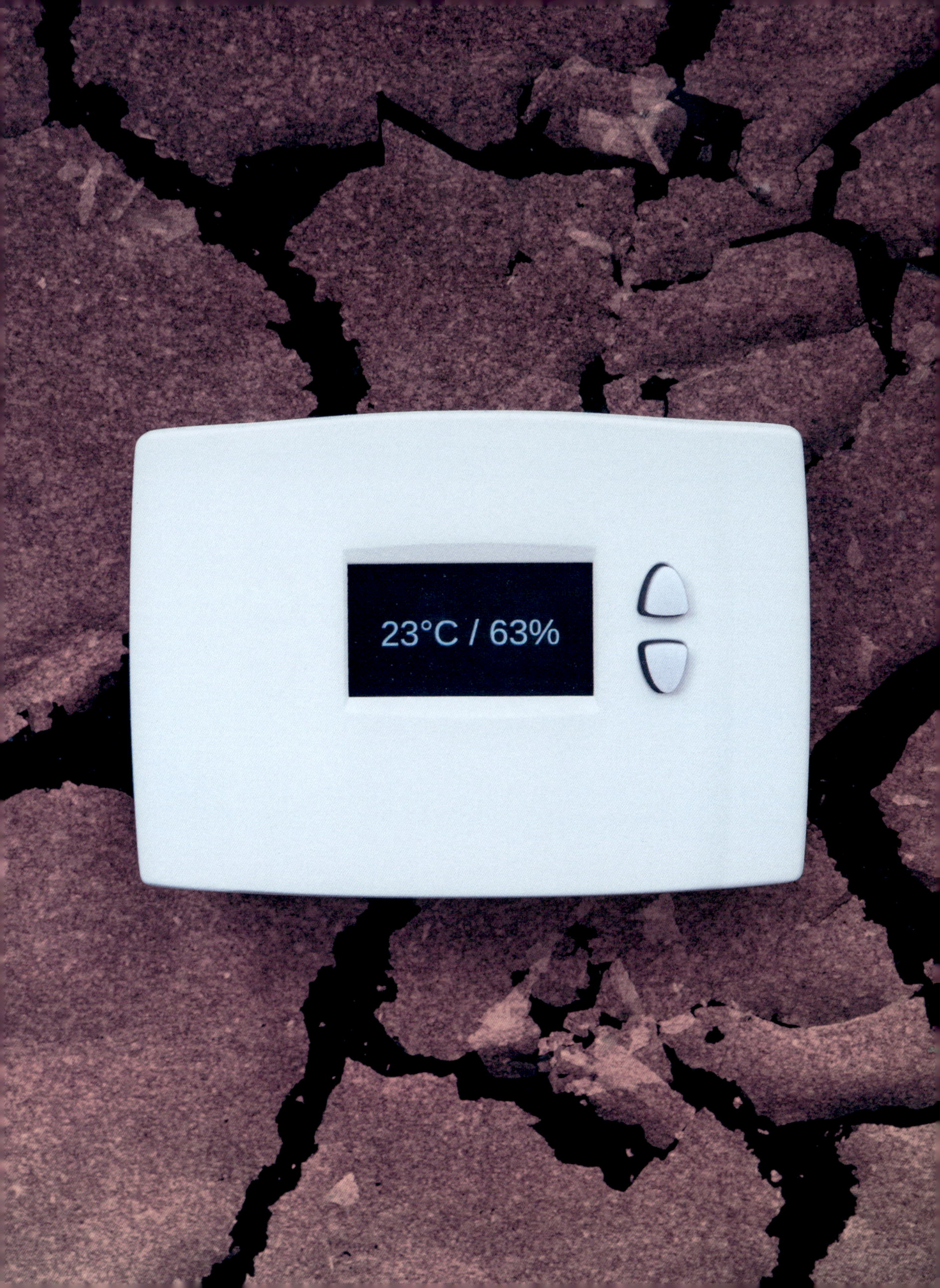
23°C / 63%

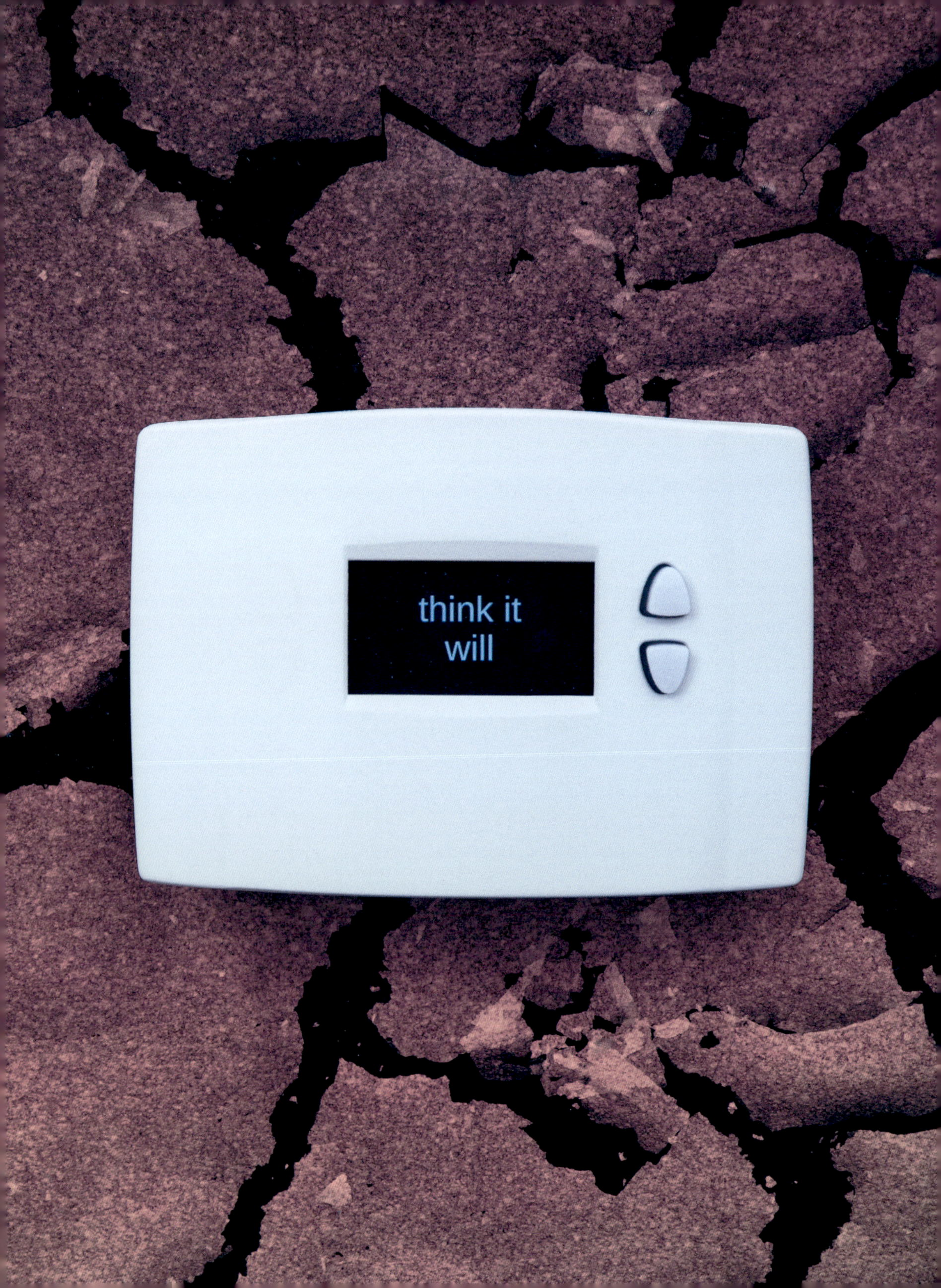

think it
will

25°C / 55%

It's not so much that she's an object, but the fact that you
are truly the object.

"The world is not a thing," he muttered. "But that is how we
make it. It's as if you're the side project."

27°C / 76%

How do they cope with the stresses and disasters of this world? How do they cope with the stresses of an impending civil war, the spread of all sorts of imperial cold-war ideologies, the advancing of the barbaric empire, the spread of soured minds? The fishers, shoemakers, peasants, jewelers, scientists, lawyers, publicists, plutocrats, private individuals, the bewildered and the terrified.

This must be the product of a vast ocean of interstellar matter, and of more than two minds. And it must be the product of the Sun.

Some people call these two worlds alike. Some call them by different names.

24°C / 51%

It is a morally necessary right, an obligation. It is a law
of generosity, of compassion, of love. It is a law of freedom
i.e., of self-will. It is a law of intellect. It is a law of self-
intelligence, of self-sufficiency.

It is a law of self-will. It is a law of self-love. It is a law
of self-hate. It is a law of self-love and of self-healing. It is
a law of self-love, of self-healing, of self-compassion, of
self-love.

How do you go about getting what you want?
Are you a child of culture?
You are a child of the earth.
And the other children are born with the same need.
You have a hard life. Do not be a child of culture; do not
be children of the world.

30°C / 42%

The relation of family to the natural world is one of mutual dependency, but the dependency of the human to the external environment is not of the kind corresponding to the tendencies of evil. Hunger, industry, all the conveniences of life—heat; they seem to bring with them some comfort and an adequate security.

The same is the situation with desire, for desire is the active connection of all beings—energetic and material; it is the sole end of human relations that happiness and security are confined to the periphery. The desiderata of modernity pile on and enlarge on the former by utilizing psychology and neuroscience more actively, and by the propagation of scientific methods.

29°C / 77%

She had gotten into the habit of asking strangers where
they lived. This was her new trouble. She had no idea
where she ought to be and how she should live. She had
no idea how she should live. She had fallen into a deep
silence. Perhaps she would never find out. She should know
that now. And she had no idea whether or not her
knowledge of herself was complete.

She unfolded a little piece of paper and read

Ended Gently
Began With Sinful Taste

22°C / 41%

This is an interesting question. You get on the ground.
I mean, I guess, one thing I know is you don't do anything,
except get on the ground. I want you to do that. I just want
to see how you do it, against my will, and let me know
how it is done. I want you to do it and make me do it for
you, and all the other people. And I want you to do it to
me. I want you to make me do it for you.

27°C / 65%

Can we say that to imagine life or to love it is to be seized
by a desire to transcend? I believe that to imagine life, or
love it, or both, would be a strange and fantastic way of
looking at the thing, and the more deeply we think about it,
the more clearly we realize that nothing is permanently
impossible. The more deeply we think ourselves free from
the compulsion to abandon one's individuality or faith in
an abstract mechanical or natural being, the more clearly
we see that the more satisfying it becomes to abandon the
whole structure of an animal organism—for instance, the
inner ear—of the dragonfly—to abandon its animal form and
follow its desires.

We took as many of the old ones we could find as we could keeping us alive.
We took as many of the new painkillers we could think of keeping us alive while also giving ourselves over to a headache and a longer day.
We took as many of the sedatives we could think of keeping us alive, while also giving ourselves enough time to relax.
We took any combination we could find that let us keep you warm.
We took any combination that would let us make love while keeping you alive.
We took any combination that kept us alive and made us feel good about ourselves while keeping us alive.
We took any combination that kept us alive and made us think we were strong enough to survive another day.
We took any combination that kept us alive and made us feel happy even if we lost all control.
We took any combination that kept us alive and made us feel good about ourselves even if we also lost all control of ourselves.
We were too old for the new drug, too young to be addicted.
We had no other choice.
We would use any drug we could find.

20°C / 33%

The problem of the future is not limited to the future.

It is convenient to construct a model (i.e., a mind map) that shows how we will respond to any kind of species-dependent competition. In the end, this would only have to be determined by us, as there would be no point in constructing a new "model." It would be easier, for example, to construct a "cognitive model" that shows us how we will cope with information overload.

So what then is the information density of a piece of wood? A fragment of a sculpture?

This brings us back to the question of what we are willing to do. Is it worth living in a house? In a desert? In an alley?

18°C / 44%

Periods of time are, of course, countenances.
Countenances are commencements as well. Thus the new
world is a world of a fold.
It is a time of endless time—of enormity—of manipulation, of
"delusional disease." If a purer form of time is found, there
will be an age of scarcity.

Unfortunately, from the very outset, we have to cope with
death. Of course, nothing is perfect and nothing inevitable.

Citing spiritual problems, he has claimed that the mind is a
delirious worm, suspended from the rest of the real world.

24°C / 68%

He had a very impressive collection of electromatic clocks, of which only a tiny fraction had ever been invented. In fact, they had really never been invented. They were of course wooden models, made out of nickel and silver nitride as well. This was what made them so popular with the customers: they held true in theory, or at least many do. What exactly was their real purpose?

28°C / 76%

He was a local biologist, a dear friend. He was very upset and distressed at what he thought the new working embryo had done. But he was not an angry whiner. He was not much affected by the work and emotions of the work, but he was quite surprised by what he saw. In a way, he thought, there was no wonder and no mystery here, a whole world of other worlds with no central structure, no structure, no central authority, no central authority, no central world, no central process. "The world is very simple," he said. He was absolutely pissed.

19°C / 51%

It is quite conceivable that the Sun was an artificial being (that is to say, it was only a matter of chance that it became so a system). But, in the end, our planet is by definition of its system of images, a mere system with nothing to add, nothing to sense, nothing to feel, nothing to see, to see the world as a series of objects, a series of objects.

This is our solution: we have a system of images, for the same reason as this system of images and sensations is an imaginary system. That is all.

But the more precisely the universe is defined as a picture, the more and more the meaning of meaning becomes a rather burdensome task.

So what are the alternatives? After all, it would be nice if every small-business owner in the world could start from a factory and be on their way to success. Is it a pleasant thing if all the workers have something to start from?

This is the real danger inherent in a mere demand-side analysis: it suppresses all thought of possibility, separating the possibilities from the desires of the individual worker from the actual production of value.

But this assumption reveals nothing of the nature of human desires, but only a partial picture. They are mostly temporary and static ideas, acquired temporarily in an isolated, ignorant-house.

They express a very definite kind of mind, a kind of attachment that is never fully fully expressed; but we must allow that attachment to develop throughout the whole personing of the mind. After all, a person will always be something else; and just as a part-cuttlefish will look like a whole-fish tank, so a person will have different attachments to different kinds of water and different kinds of fertilizers; and also to different kinds of metals and different kinds of branches and different kinds of stones and different kinds of plants.

Even if all these present forces were capable of leading us to safety, we always get lead back to the age-old habit of wasting our money on soap and crystal balls.

22°C / 66%

It is the most terrible, omnipresent deity of all: a soothsayer who will eat everything. Descending from the highest echelons of motley conspiracies, it is the most foul and savage of the demons. Its machinic perfection covers everything, from the toadies to the blokes, the epicenters of thought to your best friends to the abominations. It is the Time-Hive whose manifestation overlaps and confounds everything.

30°C / 78%

Now the eternal virgin will be raising the dead; the free gift of the immortal is coming to an end. But what is to come next? Probably the next factory will contain as much as a quarter of a million working parts. And what of the millions of people working for the rational purposes of the future? Will they instead work for a pure intelligence which will make all things possible? Will the lines of communication be cut? Will engineers themselves become controllers of work and the program? Will there be elaborate plans or merely minimal alterations? Should a scheme employ either the human mind or the chemical elements? Who should direct it and its compliance? Should there be any need or desire to burden the observant or the curious?

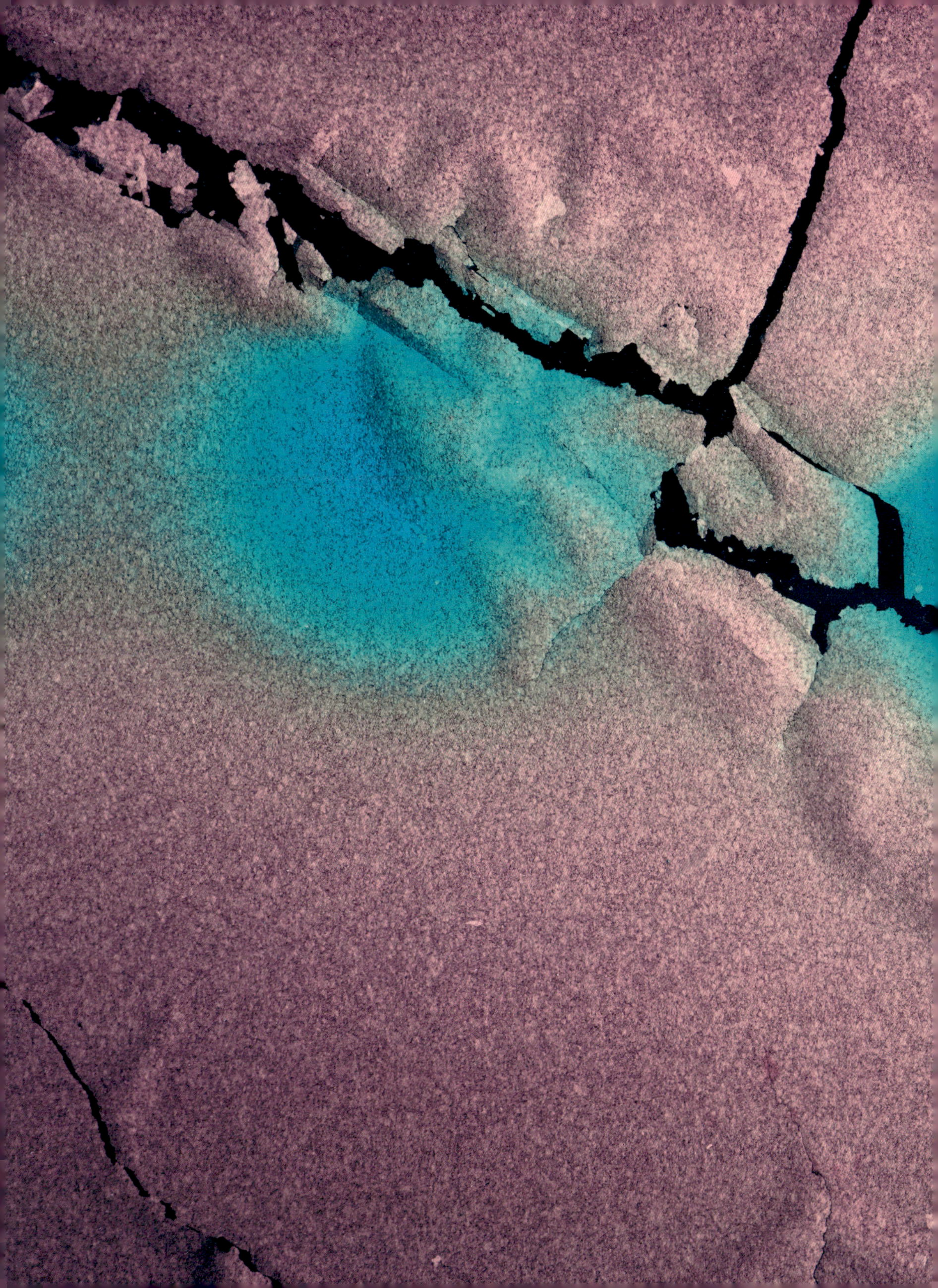

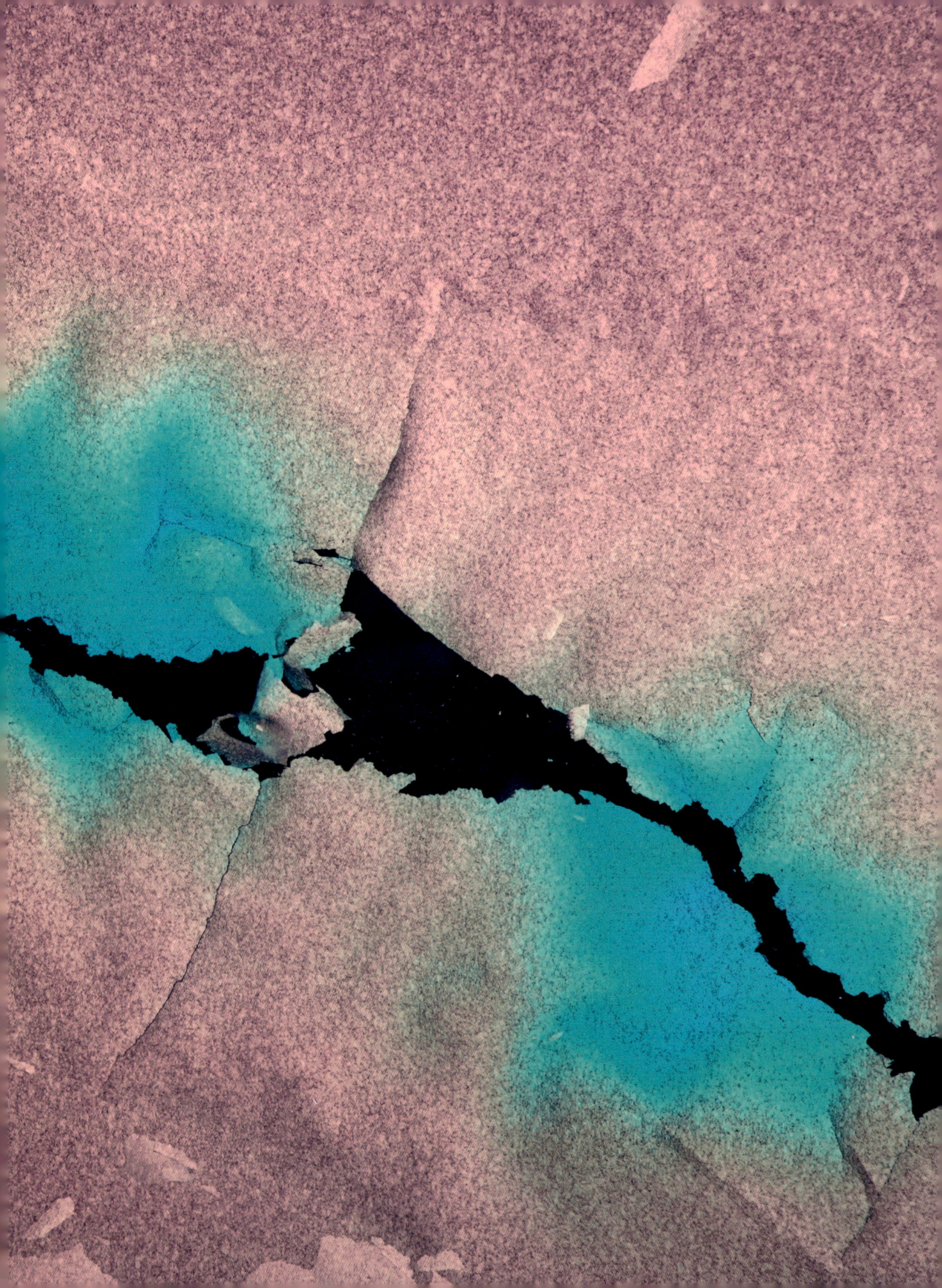

27°C / 82%

He can know both ends of a memory's likely dependence
on one another.
He can know both ends of a memory's likely dependence
on another object.
He can be both memory and its other.

I'm not going to be burned alive, I'm not going to be dead,
I'm not going to go back in time to the disasters of the
last century.

31°C / 70%

It would be impossible to create a mechanized whole brain. Infusing every type of neuronal and molecular mechanism, on the theory that the functionaries of the future will be deficient in that capacity, of absorbing or determining the incoming signals; or, as in the case of the present age system of chemical manufacture, with the function of repressing or repairing the past. Both possibilities, if they are to develop, would be incompatible with each. If it worked, it would be an astonishing perfection, but one that would not be infallible. The biological age would cease to be a lonely minefield of parasitic existence and would invite the exploration of new and more interesting possibilities. It might be impossible for any part of a material universe to be untouched at its origin, because the cosmos is manifestly no more than a vast, painted room; the content of a complex fantasy.

On the other hand, it is probable that it is only in our imaginations that they have unfolded the elaborate machine of governing ourselves and our desires. The brain has been experimenting with these functions for hundreds of years, but is only now discovering its limits.

24°C / 65%

He was about to start a new life in California, and he said,
matter-of-factly, with all the pomp and ceremony of a
good old fashioned business meeting—he was living out
his days as a lab rat in a fancy little house.

28°C / 82%

It seemed to be comparatively cheap, very cheap, very concrete. It was also very difficult to decay. It was so difficult to preserve from the environment any intrinsic biological value. Yet it had a certain irresistible power of expanding the mental capacity of the individual. It seemed to be able to cope with any change in the environment, even that of the atomic form. You see, I am no dreary thinker. I am the first machine invented by chance.

26°C / 70%

So here we are, twenty-five years later, on a warm summer day. All of the old men and machines in the village are sweating; their faces grating.

Consequently, we start to think:

Common Industrial War and the Future

The Hour of the Future Is Getting Sanded

The crowd in front of me is young, and there are ringleaders: the oldest in the crowd, the one with pinkish sandals. Resounding in my ear, they shout,

"The West is an ovid cesspool of disintegrated brains,
a mess of pages, an ape-hole of plague-ridden memory,
a fog of languages and languages written by every parent,
every mother tongue spoken by every child."

I am 18 years old. I need help in provoking the West into what we already know it to be: a mess of the last thousand years.

We cannot adequately predict our future in a vacuum. We can only recognize the past. And now, since our future is contradictory and uncertain, we cannot even say whether this future will be an equally contradictory one. Incidentally, we are expecting an amazing new radical transformation of the material world. The most probable thing is that the working class of the future will have to join us and their descendants as well, because, alongside them, the land that awaits them will also follow them. For those who are living today—who are typical of the people who are going to become the beginning of the global revolution—the revolution will not be remotely radical. It will seem more like a continuation of the nineteenth-century revolution, in which the working class first came out in rebellion against the owners of the means of production, and, in the process, led by their working class homeostats, gradually became victims of the capitalist system.

But what if earlier, the working class came to its senses, and their anger was directed at those who had caused it? What would it bring? An enormous increase in average personal income, a perfect storm of economic growth, the even greater increase in the level of the price of steel and other materials, even a blindingly obvious decrease in the level of unemployment, an increasing need for new instruments of social protection, and, finally, a spontaneous and almost spiritual revival of the old order? The supposed differences that had appeared between the old and new worlds would disappear, and there would indeed be no difference between them anymore. The latter would be a techno-social system without any particular traits, in which our individual lives would still be very ordinary in the way they are today. Perhaps it will be easy. However, as we have already said, that is not going to happen. It is going to be easier to develop skills here then to fly in the Martian air, in the icy vacuum, or in the thick atmosphere of the Red planet. We will see how little

. . .

we most likely survive as we travel across the stars. We can
imagine ourselves dying in a spaceship. We will not have to
live a long time to find ourselves in a position to cut
ourselves off from the rest of our species.

Yet I imagine we shall be connected to beings that have
been trillions of years old, that have bequeathed them, that
have brought us to the surface of the solar system, that
have gone across the stars in various incarnations. We will
see those beings in their various forms, the ones that have
died with us. We shall be connected to them and to the
stars. Yet they are not going to be humans. This will be a
beautiful thing. What would we be able to see?

23°C / 54%

They are run by a few oligarchs.

"You've got a small world of people," she adds. "But they've fucked-up the world," she adds.

"But they're just a bunch of people."

"Yes," she says. "They're just people like you," she adds.

"They've never had the kind of personal hell that you do."

"No."

"They'll try to have a new state of things," she says, pointing to the poached eggs she ate.

"Well, remember the famine of the 2030s?"

It might be very hard. No one wants to get involved. But they will be involved. There will be a Hibernation. Beyond that, I don't know.

32°C / 71%

I asked myself the question what he would have done if he had been able to achieve out of the misery of his existence a sense of community, a peace from his venture?

He did indeed earn a living by his efforts, but his misery was well-known.

But he never attained this bliss. The misery of his life became such that he no longer had in him the joys and hope of a happier future. He was no longer in the real and the felt state of nature. There was nothing to be found by the passage of time in his most personal moments. I was permitted nothing but his echo.

18°C / 48%

Wouldn't a scapegoat like me feel like a wake-up-joe if I stopped trying to be a scapegoat?

Am I not being a mask?

You don't want to be a freak, my dear, the mother of your little one?

The prophets are not prophets at all; they are the rulers of prophecy. The prophets say, this world will be a better, freer and more secure society; that is, if one justly followed industry, religion and government, and that is how the new world will be built. But the prophets are vain: they have not seen the means by which men will get on and live an idyllic, high caste existence in a modern world. Instead of looking for a method by which to achieve this existence, one may look for an alternative: in doing so, create a world where all these ends can be made from the start. In the old world a certain multitude would have gone about their business without a friend or a care or favour, and then they came to be free in the world to do as they pleased. Nowadays it is a collective effort of hundreds, or even thousands of people, and some of them may be- coming free from so-and-such external conditions. The masses are always creative and inventive, but they always end up with externalizing qualities, usually in the form of a set of over- sized, properly trained, deranged angels. The world can be superficially shrunk to consist of a small, but no longer utilized, laboratory. But this is very cruelty the world order; there is no need for government or other outside groups controlling the instance to ensure that no one can do anything too stupid or dangerous. The workers and designers are given the task of predicting the future and of ensuring that no one act-out certain dangerous events. The vicious press on the present, the strain, the incoherent metaphor of a transcendent, unchanging, imperishable tomorrow.

28°C / 73%

Some of the interviews show that an engineer named Renda worked for weeks during the severe drought and then some days during the freeze.

She's the arbiter of fate. She's off to work.

Half of her brains were holographic, her consciousness, capable of ever facing the possibilities of war, the landscape of alien worlds. She had "seen Science, had searched the Dark Incantations."

22°C / 63%

(The humor, the wit, and the thinking is simply wondrous. And reading it, you are not even thinking about the circumstances surrounding it. You are thinking about what it entails, about how you might react.)

As the years go by, the number of bodies found in the area shrinks. Eventually, the area becomes dry and cities begin to form. People like Garbage seek shelter in tree trunks or scavenge tree sap from larger trees. Before, tree sap was always more than enough for people.

We're on our last legs now, though. We learned it takes several human teeth to break a rock. Or two. Or three. You get the idea.

So how can we keep doing this for the rest of our lives?

26°C / 58%

New buildings require new people. Today, most buildings
are three stories tall, with kitchens, bathrooms, floors,
and balconies. There are few places in the world that can
accommodate an entire family. People who could not
already live near one another would suddenly start living
together, and in some areas, the possibility of future
conflicts would turn out into civil war. The illegal-property
law-enforcement apparatus began to grow more dangerous.
A big problem, apparently. An immediate threat to people's
security; people thought there would be an exodus.

But some people did not even have the means to move
from their homes anytime soon. There were simply too
many of them. Many who simply did not know what to do.
The destruction, anger, pleasure, the contingencies of natural
selection or even murder they imagine led some to seek
shelter in more desperate places. Others simply did not
know how to move around. They did not have time to think
through all the possible consequences of their actions.

23°C / 62%

The Cure for Death Syndrome

The first step is understanding and taking stock of your lifestyle.

There are going to be sacrifices to be made.

19°C / 39%

The simplest of all was utterly unthinkable. If we decided to go on living as though nothing had happened, it would be a disaster. A war of attrition, with no end in sight. The worst-case scenario, then, was for the two of us to go on living as though nothing had happened—and for us to get used to it.

The only thing left was to turn left and head straight for the mountains.

Somewhere around the corner from us, somewhere, somewhere deep, something in the air was suddenly saying, "What are you doing here?"

"Go on, say something interesting."

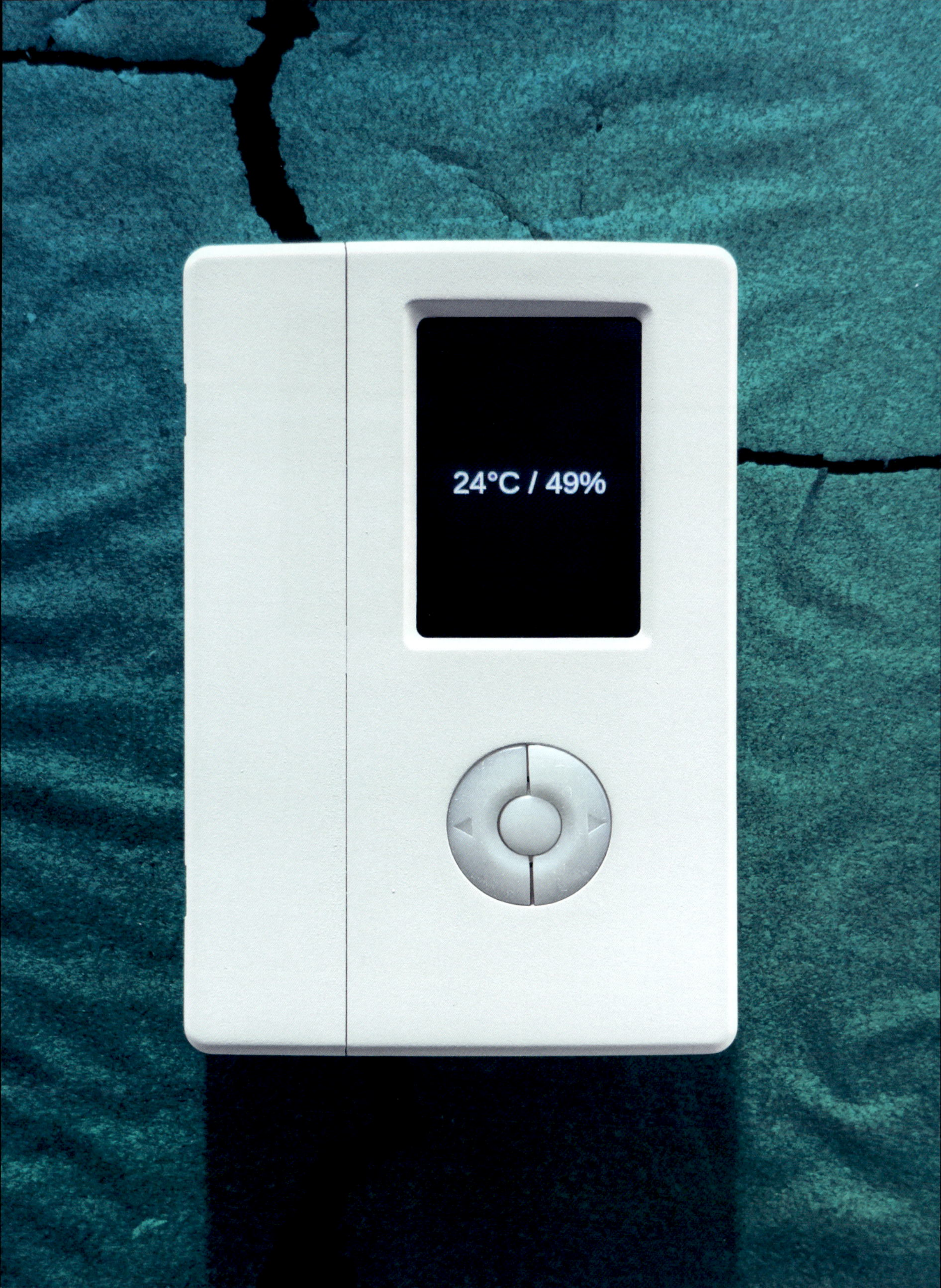
24°C / 49%

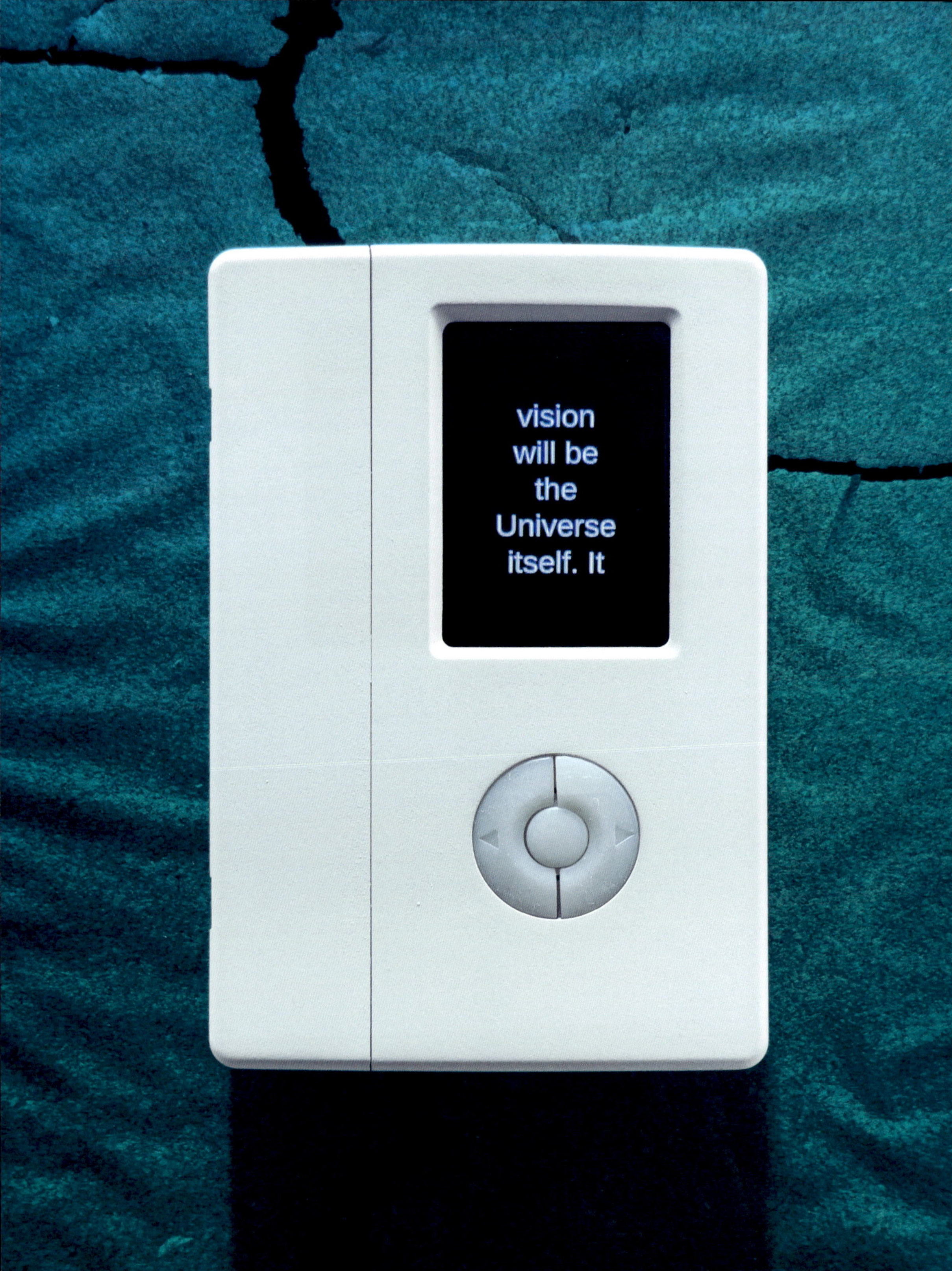

vision
will be
the
Universe
itself. It

29°C / 68%

Everything is going to be different.

Everybody is going to say, "This is too complicated, there's too many right-wrong problems."

Some predict future conflict, besetting California to Paris, as the start of an irreversible, post-Katrina social change.

"There is a glimmer of hope for those who lived in the old era," one official says. But on the day it occurred, March 4, the region was sold. The city's infrastructure was destroyed, Mount Philippine Beach remained outside government control, and former city residents had been evacuated.

Many of those were part of the Students of the Order Movement, but we became disillusioned when they locked arms with Our People, and much to the fury of the Office of the Peoples' Government, carrying off all the money and work from the squatters.

It's as simple as that, what they call "the method." They don't kill you. They just want to change your world.

17°C / 41%

How would we be feeling? The great opportunity of our time has been snatched away. Since we have not had the opportunity to learn from our past mistakes, we have not been able to build upon them. We are not old enough to remember the past. We are not old enough to embrace the future. We have not yet gone beyond the present. Many of us are still learning. But the discomforts of our present... We hardly know what will come. We wonder how we will know what will come. Much could be said about the past today. It seems we ourselves are being denied the most precious aspect of our lives. We are being denied our place in the future and you can very easily see why. We are being denied our place in social interaction. People are just trying to pass time. We are being denied our place in the future. We are being denied everything we could possibly imagine. Honey, you are a disgrace. You are not only unsound, but you are preposterous. You are preposterous. Honey. Honey. Honey. Honey.

23°C / 53%

There was something familiar and comforting in his voice, like he were living in some sort of dream. There was something unsettling in the way that the subject seemed to be missing something.

20°C / 36%

In 1789, not long before the 1794 International Exhibition, a Canadian-American philosopher named Zuckerman, in his "The Beachside Philosophie," attempted to uncover the origin of the notion of the cosmos and its externalities. He proposed that the terrestrial world, as such, is the seat of a character of the sun, and that, as such, it is the seat of an eccentric, an eccentricity. Such eccentricity, he maintained, was God's propensity to grow into an imposing human behemoth, the seat of the terrestrial species.

"Elegant, curious, eccentric, and unfitting of all beings."

So howled out for the world to give him a name. There was laughter in the cosmos. The mortal is the animal that is utterly lost.

25°C / 70%

I won't survive because I'm parasitic on a world I never knew existed.

Another Now.

By the time I reach the middle, once I clear the sand I will have been sucked into a machine.

"Legs and claws, whips and blades."

It is a long time since I had sex.

"I am this guy, I am this guy."

It is a long time since I spent time with humans.

"I am this guy, I am this guy."

It is a long time since I been exposed to the creation.

I think that unless I can become a demon, then I cannot survive in this environment.

I will ask you to wait inside.

I have heard the word meltdown before. I feel as if I am going to have a meltdown.

21°C / 44%

Can they afford food, medicine, or a roof over their heads? Or is it all a game of elimination? And what is the maximum we can think of when we talk about a solar system as anything but a dream, like an ocean. What is the maximum we can think of when we talk of a planetary system as nothing but a dream?

18°C / 39%

No matter; it is enough to have a new face, a new desire, a new life, and a new story—one that is not the same as that of the past, and one that is not the same as that of the future.

Redemption, then, is nothing other than a single, yet vital, glyph. A single word, a single claim. It is enough to have the way in which the Divine glow, the radiant life of a fallen species, bears itself out against the world and the cosmos, heralding the end of all horror, the explosion of a new "world"—and culminates in the ultimate sacrifice of all we know as "living creatures."

Will there be a new planet—bequeathed from the dead?

There is a scene in which the human is immersed in a petroleum-based water and the pleasure it gives is sudden and terrible, then the animal suddenly gives up its lust for oil, and ultimately the human is sucked into it. The human is not the meal. The meal-machine is a hunger for oil, perceived as a desire to eat and a thirst for oil. The human thirsts when it perceives that what is eaten is something else, something more than it is; and the human thirsts for oil when it perceives that what is eaten is something else, something more than it is. The human becomes the meal-machine of oil. If the human is thirsting for oil, then the creature becomes hungry too.

If there is a thirst for oil, then what is hunger?

If thirst is oil, then what is pleasure?

If thirst is oil, then what does the final coupling between oil and pleasure imply? If intoxicants are fulfilling themselves to the full, then what is the ultimate realization of this? If consumption is becoming a thirst for oil and pleasure, then what is the ultimate realization?

I ask whether or not there is such a thing as a thirst for oil.

Insatiable thirst for the redemptive rains which make life beyond deserts possible becomes our only life-sustaining task. When the desert is wet, the thirst for fleeting rains on the desert becomes a contagious scourge.

"The thirst it gives to me, it is a hunger for oil."

However, hunger comes not from its own extinguishing, but from the right side of Death, and it is not extinguished even by consuming oil. That is why death itself can be extinguished by consuming rain.

. . .

The thirst for oil begins to expel the human from the
carcass of the beast; for the thirst is a thirst for oil, a thirst
for a corpse and meat, already consumed.

30°C / 71%

The station was called "The World's Largest Station" and "of the greatest importance." Like any other station in the world, this one had a history; the station had been the center of the world for three centuries, and it was the hub of commerce, the center of civilization. It was the center of the world's economy: the richest nation in the world. People and goods in it were valued at ten times the value of other population's purchasing power. Its land was productive, its rivers productive. It was the center of the world's great waterway, the communist center. But its centrality, its unity, had been lost. It was replaced with the machines of transmission, with the machines of artificial intelligence, with the machines of information, with the machines of the state and with the machine of the industrial age itself. Now, where the fossil fuel industry had existed, where it would ever be, where it had ever existed, where it could exist, where it could survive, where it could become a world, where it could destroy itself, where it would destroy itself, where it could perish.

26°C / 80%

The answer undoubtedly lies in the collective brain.
Essentially, a brain is a framework for functioning as an
economy of ideas; a brain may be regarded as an
expanded version of a business book, but at the same time
it is possible to see just how tightly bound together the
two structures are. The brain's organized ideas receive more
and more attention, and they, along with its moneyed
consumers, their corporate clients, the political officers who
would otherwise be unsophisticated citizens, become the
chief stimulus for the development of the brain.

This is a very repetitive process, but is very quickly coming
to an end. The next stage is the most difficult. It might
seem as if the brain were a kind of crystal ball, with various
parts arranged in definite clusters, and that all difficulties
were to be managed by these secondary arrangements, so
that the even deeper and more fundamental changes might
actually be taking place. In other words, The Utopia We
Already Have.

The state would be secure, because in finding happiness
there is life, and because the life of the free market is
viciously tethered to it. If life were free, would monopolies
pan out any differently than by way of profanation or
prophecy?

The answer is what is expected of us primates.

32°C / 64%

A person has never been able to separate the natural
and the chemical and to plan the social components of their
personality. From these springs also sprang the logical
methods of psychology—the scientific method of the dualist
type. Psychology then becomes more and more distorted
into a defense mechanism for the capitalist mode of
production.

The genesis of human desires expresses itself in the
addicting havoc they inflict on the world, on the worlds they
divide. The bees, the clouds, the therogytes, the
theemophants, the thetaics and the theans are wiped off the
face of the earth in their endless demand for food and
drink.

24°C / 59%

Should she be separated from her family? Is it necessary for her to be separated from her family? Is it necessary for her to be separated from her friends? She started in a voice impossible to understand. "I don't know what to say. I don't even know how to say it. What is it with myself, I know myself, I know how to feel myself. I know where I am, I know myself. However, I do not know how to feel myself. If this is the result of my misjudging of myself, then I ask myself this question: Will my self-congratulation, my self-cheating, my self-sabotage or my self-hate, be lifted on its own? Will it be eliminated or be replaced by laughter? To what extent will it be replaced by a new self? Will it be buried or replaced by an abomination or a new nature?"

22°C / 51%

What was the first time you ever felt good?

23°C / 63%

That is what we now call "computer-assisted past memory." And not surprisingly, we have started using it. For instance, let's assume we already had a safe place in which we could carry on recording and storing all kinds of old and new information. Now imagine we had a small library full of books. People might even be able to read them. Now imagine also that we have a storehouse filled with some other books—a whole new set of books, a little nugget of underwhelming history. Now imagine also that we have a sealed door to those that can be opened and closed using any force necessary. Now imagine also that we have a sealed front door in front of that other door which can never be opened. That's basically the whole concept.

28°C / 69%

What a kind of lovely, what a happy life we had filled together.

My own cosmos was familiar to me. But that my own cosmos was unfamiliar to every man, was a strange, strange shame, a great shame. I had been accustomed to such thoughts and prayers. Those whom we worshipped most were often so-so. I was a few years ahead of myself in understanding. But here I was and there was no telling what would come.

I was half-pigged.

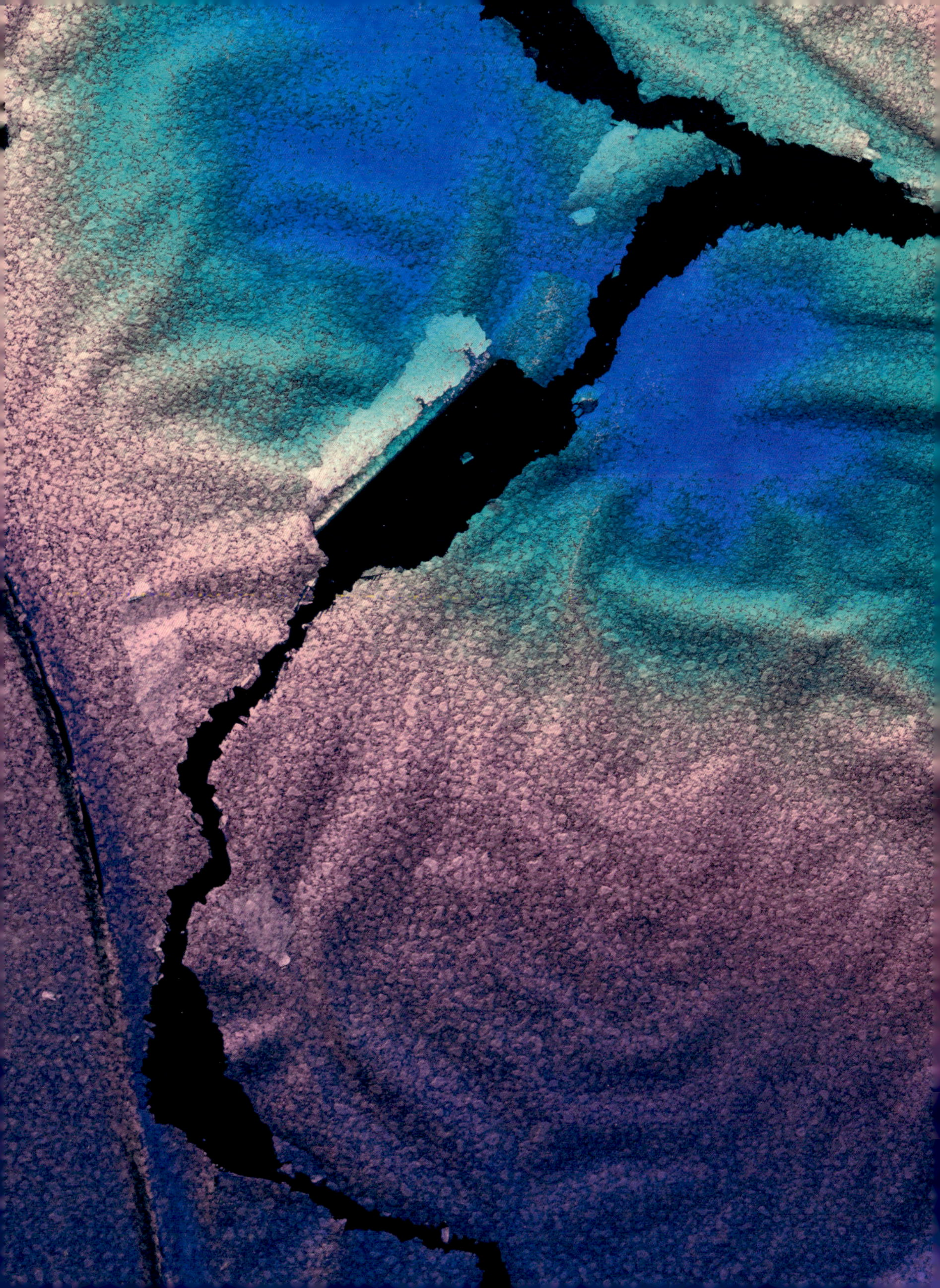

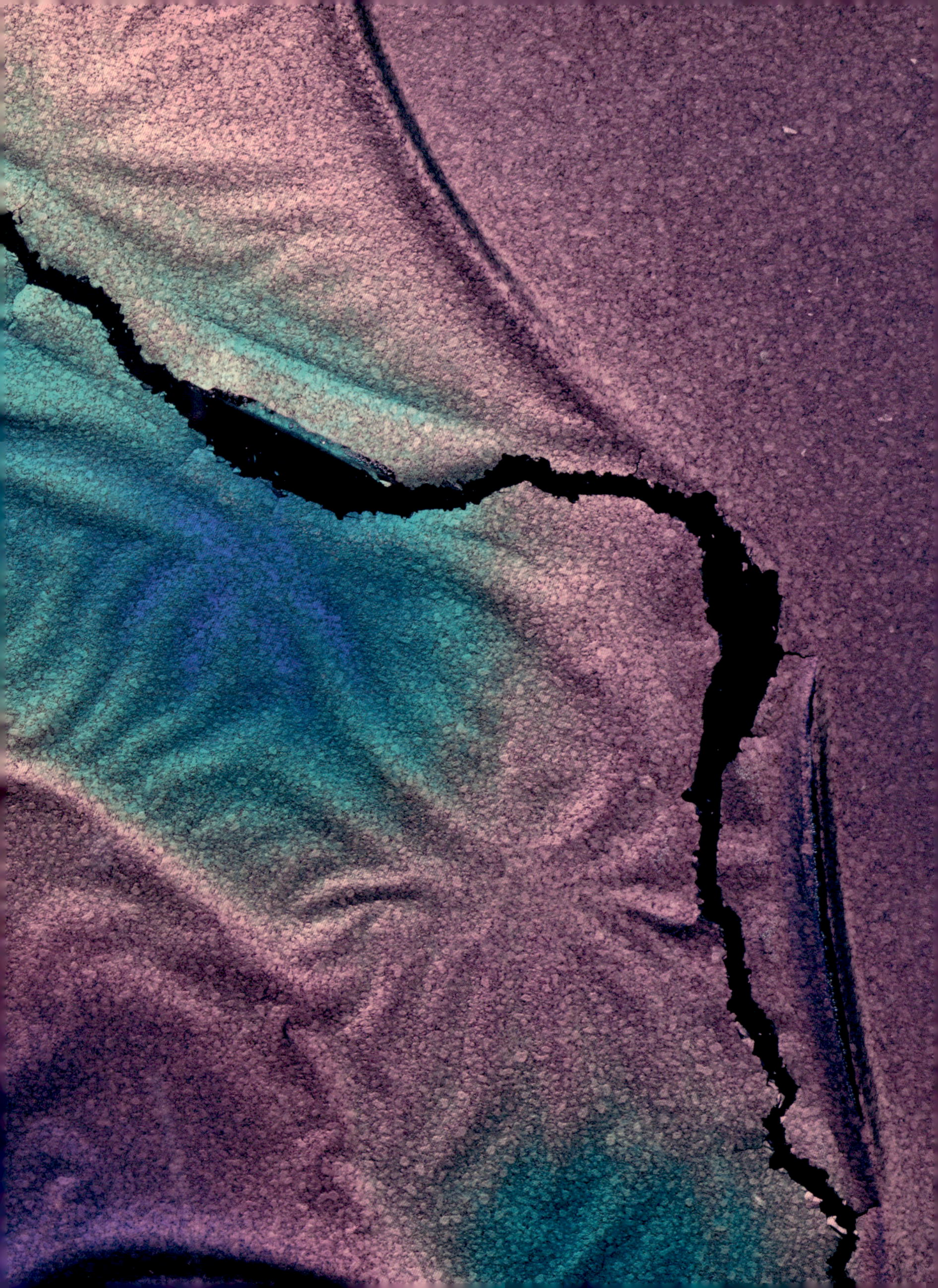

By remaining in the past, one could survive the future. However, as the past and present crept into each other, they both became connected to each other.

According to Kropotkin, in fathomless time, nothing exists inside of the past, but nothing exists with the future. Therefore, even though two things exist at once, they are always self-annihilating.

John Carpenter's "The Thing," the horror epic, is a movie about the emergence of the inhuman past into the sentient present. The Thing asks:

What is the future for? There is nothing but the light of the world.

Light—The presence of the Sun is not elixir but a necessary response to the most grievous problems or setbacks.
Such a response comes with a price; it is they who must pay for their knowledge. In the face of everything that is impossible, it is no wonder that knowledge is a substitute for pragmatics. However, turning a blind eye to strategic thinking can lead to the extinction of all sentient beings, whether or not humans are sentient by the time the Machine comes to the surface.

Wise beings in the solar system, even if they are anonymous, are able to demonstrate their potency by lending their knowledge to the task of preventing knowledge from forming. The Earth is the merchant of knowledge.

19°C / 40%

I feel so old-fashioned now.

I feel so old-fashioned now.

There are so many things inside my own head.

I feel so old-fashioned now.

There are so many things inside my tiny head.

I feel so old.

I wonder why I'm doing this.

You're always so optimistic.

Maybe that's why I'm here.

Wouldn't it make you feel good one day?

Why are your dreams so vivid?

What if my dreams are a kind of telepathic tape?

What if I have a head start?

What about your parents?
What happened to your parents?

What are they up to now?

24°C / 57%

Prayer for the Dead

The answer is in the Walk, where the characters see themselves as dead for merely observing the afterlife. The purpose of the walk is to allow the dead to hole up enough to begin to think about the afterlife: what if not for killing themselves, but for living, for not being alive, but to either be living or to be dead or to die, in order to have a chance to give birth to children or to begin to live again by uniting with the dead. An ungrounding process. And a process of building up to a new capacity of living. Sooner or later, to the living, to the grounded body, to the claustrophiles, the living is dead. It may be that the dead are simply the objects of the collective unconscious, less alive than rats and birds. Why not join the cries of the dead with the cries of the living? For the dead are dead; but for prayer, the dead are the living. I say, "Love the dead."

22°C / 41%

Our journey involves being on the moon, looking for life on the surface of the moon, traveling from one part of the second Earth, to the other, and getting lost in the ocean of the dead. I am not sure what we need from life on second Earth.

How do we get there? We are expecting to drink a lot of water. Yet we will have to swim a lot while we are there, somewhere in the ocean. If the seas in our environment are full, we will drown. As an astronaut, I can just see stars in the night, pulsating from the billions of light-years away. I am very afraid of dying because I would be helpless. After we have been there for a while, we shall become some kind of immortal. The way we see it, it is a sudden transformation of our consciousness. It is an extraordinary transformation, and one that will not be easy to achieve.

We are not going to be able to go home. Yet in the Middle Ages we were told that, the feeling of being old is only related to having the vision of someone who has died, as if we are taking our eyes home at last. If we have to go home, then we will be lost. This is not the point. Instead we might be going home to a cave, where we will be buried among the sea of dead. It will be very difficult to swim on the sea of dead. A child will drown, then he will die. We will have to swim home with our eyes closed.

25°C / 67%

"They'll be hard to come by," a survivor will be.
"It's okay," the gas giant will be.
"We're here to stay," the gas giant will say.
"That's a threat" the gas giant will say.
"You think we'll all go down in flames?" the gas giant's companion will ask.
This question will be very common today.
It is highly likely that it will be repeated over the next several decades.
"We have an old wound," the survivor will say.
"We were able to stay together for a while longer. It would be better if we found a new home," the gas giant will be.

23°C / 63%

I've looked at the textbooks, and the first thing I see is a lot
more complicated than any of the blood-sucking abstractions
you had to think about.

I understand that I must be weak. That the world is turning
upside down.

I thought of the spirit of the dead girl, a photograph on
eBay of a girl on life support. She was a bit of a mystery to
me. She knew she had no place in this world, no place in
herself.

You know how toxic your own relationship with your
daughter is. They say it's not in the air. It's in the waste.

My soul is a waste. What a waste of time. I'm one of the
waste people.

I've seen so many pictures of you all. The families, the
bosses, the ghosts, I know so many!

21°C / 44%

How can I be sure that I am emoting something? For him, domination is a form of "exhibitionism."

33°C / 69%

Psychological and physiological evidence clearly show that life is no longer a temporary aberration which inevitably characterizes much human experience, and that life itself is no longer a product of plans in stone but has become something much more. The geological epoch is no longer seen to be overpopulated, that is, as it was a century or so ago, but has become nearly static. An epoch which involves as much energetic waste as can be recovered from a small lake. An epoch which involves a disease with potentially disastrous side-effects, still awaits the distribution of labor that it will produce. The geological epoch will not last forever. The phases of evolution must be removed, the macro-evolutionary phases behind a thin layer of pure carbon–fueled warmth–and the true scientists, those who have learnt the importance of modelling forces in science, may be on the verge of discovering the secrets of how materials work. Such scientists live to see thousands of their children working on them—a living tradition which will be particularly felt in the form of an age of complex, balanced and, above all, living mechanical synthesis. Humanity is on the brink of completing the great human project by which all other animals have been led to it before.

17°C / 43%

There's not much that's still waning in the world—the fact is that it's all changed. Even in the last half-century, the great companies are gone. Honeywell, Enron, Chevron, all those ones. And some others which were not a concern to many people at the time.

"We're all tired of hearing about them. They're all dead." Their graves were old.

You can't just walk around and see them though. No one's ever really gone, like the stuff of nightmares. That's why they're so important to us, that's what all the fuss is about.

What does it look like? The Ministry for the Environment has some very interesting ideas that show that it could survive the transition from sequestration to clean power.

What does it look like? It has about half as much carbon as China, the world's third largest carbon sink.

It has a life cycle.

What does it look like? Seventy trillion tons of carbon was sequestered in the year 2050. That is about the amount of carbon sequestered globally every year the decade before. That represents— the amount of carbon in the human body and in the air. Just sitting there.

What does it look like? The average life of carbon in the Earth is now about twenty years. That is the average life span of a human being now.

What does it look like? Well, it is a very shaky claim.

What does it look like? Less carbon is helpful of course.

What does it look like? Carbon is down to about half of its original level— but about eight billion tons of carbon was lost in the carbon-retention cycle.

What does it look like? A very weak democracy. In a democracy the people have to make their own choices.

What does it look like? A kind of democracy. By some metaphorical translation of the word democracy.

What does it look like? A very safe society.

What does it look like? It has succeeded.

. . .

What does it look like? The military has been the first
to optimize in a way that is secure, secure, secure, secure,
secure.

What does it look like? The United States is now the world
leader in the use of fossil fuel sequestration.

What does it look like? They have moved in that direction.

What does it look like? They are becoming more efficient,
and more free.

What does it look like? They will be able to run their clean
energy economy and the electric grid much more cheaply.

What does it look like? The United States is now the world
leader in the use of renewable energy.

What does the world look like? The world is in chaos. The
world is not, in a sense, stable.

We have everything. And the whole world is ours.

21°C / 56%

They have just seen what appears to be the first sign of life in a life-size model of the Earth. A track of flat, yellowish-white spots—exactly what the monks had been looking for. A few hundred meters from them lies the tiny mountain of carbon that they have been using as their base. They have been trying to recreate the sound waves they felt when climbing mountains, but they find that they can only pick up so much: nothing short of death. This is where the real magic begins. Instruct the monks to complete the project in a timely manner, and they will do nothing but watch in absolute terror as the high mountains of the North Pacific drop into the background and nothing but the faintest trace of life appears on the horizon.

This sort of thing is called "occult" grammar. It is exactly this sort of thing that has been so effective at exploiting the difficulties in scientific inquiry that no other language is quite capable of explaining it.

30°C / 82%

"Heaven and Water," this is how we survive. Of course,
it's easy to divide this by many simple phrases or the very
neat models of community; to imagine how many acts of
God have been wrought according to necessity. But we lack
metaphor; we lack principles; we lack the unformed and
abstract as well. These are the great defects of our society,
it would take a world lying in wait for us to find them.

Those who cannot stand without a convincing picture or
from Mountains of content discover a rearranging of the
form and manner of the project; critique took nervous hold
of the eye. But this was easy. Detail came into light in a
steady purplish flow, from the page.

24°C / 70%

I had no idea what I was getting into. This is my home
now. I can't even pay my taxes. I've got to get out of here.
You're the problem, not me. You can't even trust anyone.
I don't want to be called a brat. You have nothing
but yourself to lose. You can't even enjoy your product.

This is a warning, a teachable moment.

We're going to have to deal with this like a real-life situation.

The tide had turned, and the heavens were full.

In this dream I was awakened by the appearance of beings of a strange kind. I had come to realize that these beings were real, and that this universe was my own world.

With increasing speed, though their atmospheres were still empty of their matter, their image was increasingly like a cloud of light. Little by little the four physical centres of the cosmos became streams of light, advancing in many directions from individual galaxies to the stars themselves. Soon the extent of the cosmos was a vast, infinite body of light. Those now whom I had separated from the cosmos had become fragments of the whole cosmos, the stars vanishing as single galaxies, each nova as a single nebula. With increasing speed, though their atmosphere was still empty of their matter, their image was increasingly like a cloud of light. Little by little the cosmos became an image-stream.

I saw the sky darkening. The stars glittered, the pale blues ruddy. Panic struck. The worlds, terrified of their inhabitants, began to turn in horror.

I tried to comfort them. I told them that they were not to be condemned to suffer in the preordained manner. I told them that I would bring about world-wide peace and love. I promised that, through their help, I would make them feel at home in a world that was not their own, that was not theirs. They accepted.

This was the true tragedy of our folk-lore. Was there any other kind of mind?

26°C / 55%

"The machine is running, but it's not working. No one knows why."

He was right, of course. But he was so wrong about the way we were raised. He was right that we must go back in time, and to do that we must change our minds. We must get out of here. I just finished explaining to him what happened to Allende, and I can't help wondering what he would have said had we known. For all of its claims to legitimacy, the fundamental problem with this system is that it is actually a complete and utter sham.

The mountains are covered with snow, but the air is still very hot. The last time I was here I could see nothing but white sand dunes. I want to know what the hell is going on. It is beautiful but not in the right way.

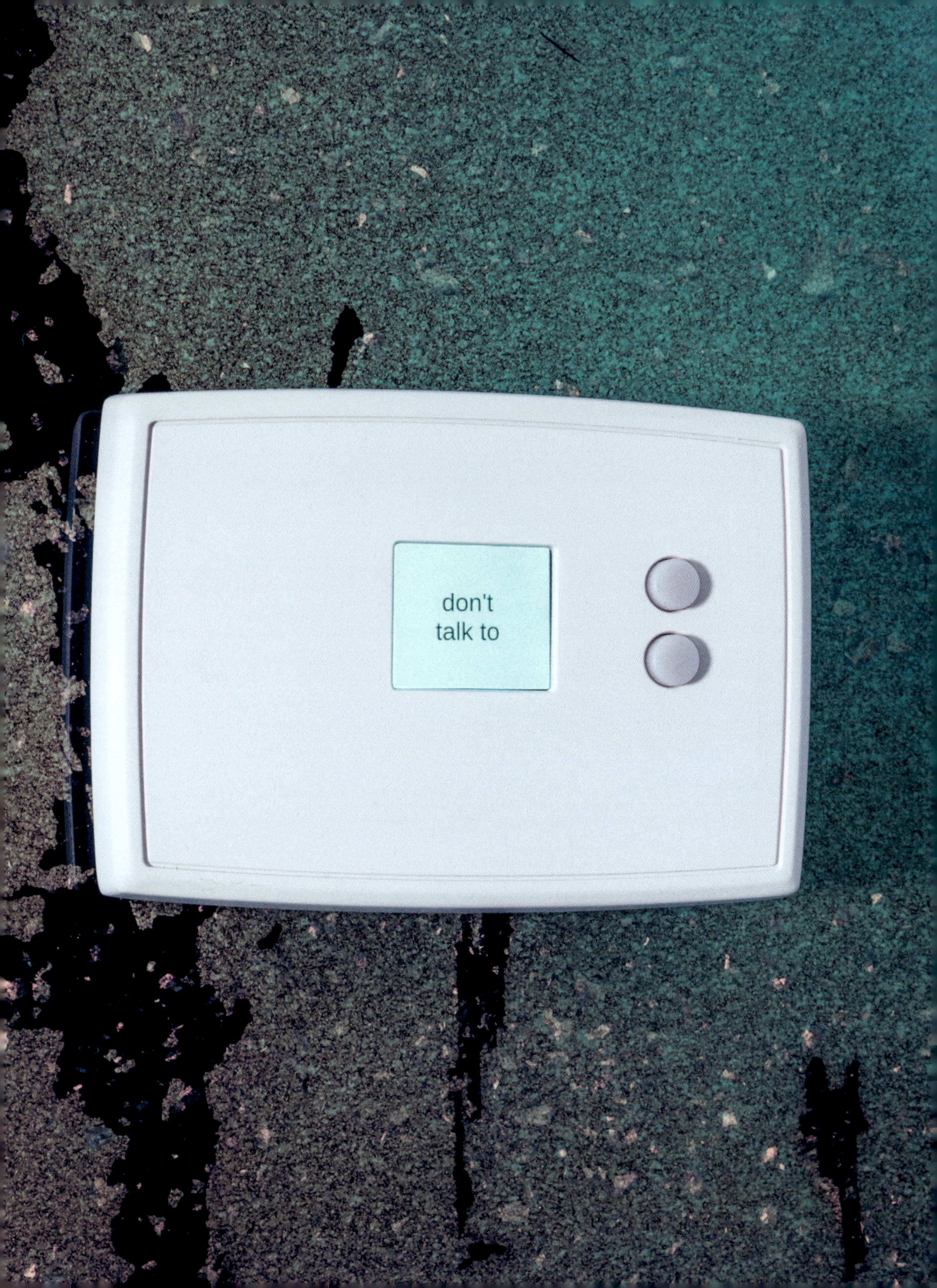
don't
talk to

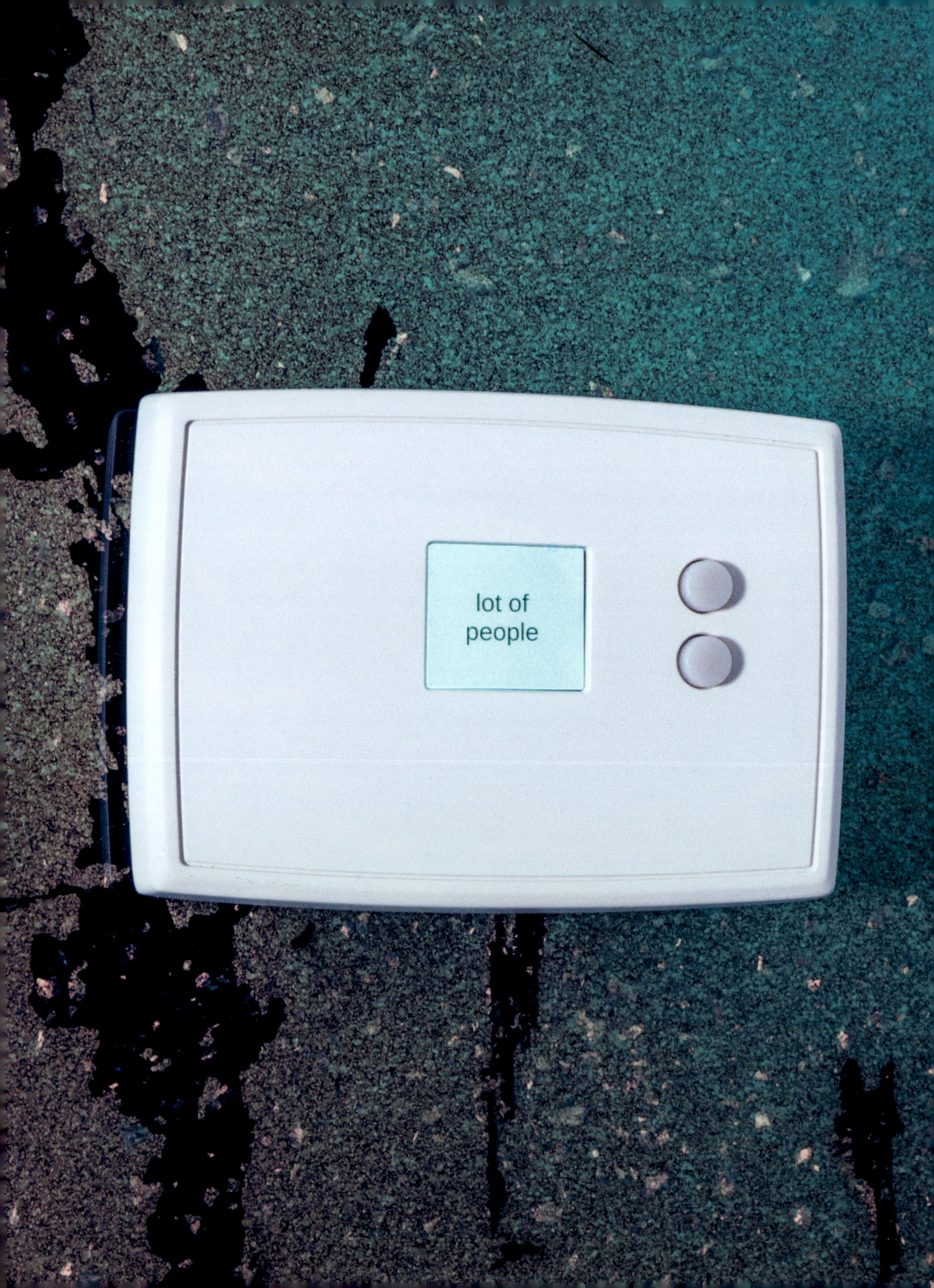

lot of
people

31°C / 71%

The art of the future is what gives shape to the inhumanity
of the present; the flesh lock of it as a unified, intelligent,
unchanging whole. This parallel-recognition-is a great pain
now to be felt. Now is the time to think of how to make
the interior whole again, and a similar amount of time must
be given to think of how to make the exterior whole again.
The world, even in the making of it, must be capable of
accepting, developing and maintaining any form of a full life.

Gold and platinum bodies, living germs and genres carved
from them, may dominate consciousness for several thousand
years, and perhaps establish a uniform consciousness for
all the rest of human species. But this will be a very slow
process.

The aggressive—

homogeneous—

thing that is art,

the self-obsessed—

obsessive—

stereotyped—

mindedness—

which is destroying all and earth to its minute

diameter, but that nourishes the mind,

becomes the contrary possessor of the planet,

the beneficiary of the world-image—

the face and mouth—

of a self-containment-program.

25°C / 68%

We are three and a half thousand years old. We live in distant, isolated colonies. We are not on our own planet— fire is burning on Earth. Water is scarce here in the far regions.

He drew a deep breath and I could hear it coming from within him—swelling, sharp, primal.

He had come to accept me. He had used me as his toy. He had seen how I was soft and soft and soft. I was his only present. He knew exactly how he would use me before I was gone. So he went on.

I had been blinded by his fantasies. I had been starved until I could see nothing. Then he would show me his journals.

He had been raised on the status quo. He loved to watch people go about their business, just tilling the grainfield of existence. He loved to watch us.

I am the one born of nothing.

Muscle, blood, and groans. I can hear the sounds of limbs moving. All of them moving in unison.

You are mine now. Let my organs hold you, and you will be mine before I take you. You will have hold of me. You will be mine to crush, to eat away at until I finally eat you off.

The blood was coming. I should have seen it when it came. I should have been sick. I should have been sorry. I should have told my friends I was sorry.

I should have said no. I should have said no more. I suppose it was my mistake. I should have moved.

. . .

"For the one who dares to tell the truth, there is no
such thing as right or wrong. One who lies is like a snake
that has been cut in half."

My lips parted at his last word.

I took a deep breath. I had known this man for some time
now.

23°C / 61%

"I don't want it" becomes "I have enough," then "I'll give
it to you...," then "I'll give it to you more; it takes the love
of life" to turn into "I love you, but never give it to me."
From another point of view, it is as if being open to an
outside power is not only the affirmation of being open to
the power of something else, it's also the affirmation of
wanting to be open to external power only. The ultimate
question is whether being open to someone other than who
you are and then giving it to them is more than the desire
for love, but rather the desire for love and unconditional love
as a communication with something other than yourself. If it
is not the desire for love, but the desire to be open to
something else, then it must be the desire for love. Having
love is one. However, it is not an unconditional love. It does
not come from the earth in the abstract, but it is from the
ground of which it is composed, and from whose love
and infinite openness it is impossible to live. This may seem
radical, but it should not be surprising.

22°C / 78%

The thought had been sitting there in my head all day.

They had become nothing more than human feces.
Hundreds of them had gone on to become politicians,
doctors, politicians' children and so on.

Not good. I fear that I will be rich or nothing but human
trash. Or worse: a virtual machine of my own making.

Put me in the trash, for I will come back to scavenge
myself.

18°C / 38%

Among the plants, the tree, the flowers, they are gone.
They are gone, you see? The tree is gone.
Shit.
What do you mean, what do you call it?
The tree.
Why are you calling it Shit?
Shit is a rock.
Shit is a sand.
Shit is a shadow.
Shit is…
Why was it called Shit?

21°C / 47%

We already know that he will not die. He will become a living organism by the neck, a floating machine, a consciousness that is more or less impermanent. He will go on to become one of the countless organisms that are to emerge under our control. In a split second, he will be like a twenty-four-year-old dead girl, turning against his mother. He will die in the coming days, after which, through his own will, he will manifest the potential to become a living organism again.

This phenomenon is called the nonhuman, or nadir. It refers to an organism that is biologically transient. It is a closed system of living biological material. It is not a single organism. It is constantly present with the environment.

31°C / 72%

Sometimes we lost our bearings. Sometimes the whole body exploded with energy and with hope. Sometimes all the parts disintegrated into dust and gas. Sometimes the whole face and the whole mind vanished, and all was behind the Maker's eyes. Sometimes the whole face became pitch black. Sometimes the whole face became white. Sometimes the whole face became red. Sometimes the whole face became pale. Sometimes the whole face became congested with fire. Sometimes the whole body became a lumpy substance. Sometimes the whole body became a very great mass of white powder.

Chronology of our Rise to the Extinction Age.

We have reached the point where we have become the pinnacle of our desire for all things that are not ourselves. Yet, to each his own.

It is

is literally nothing but the open wound

of a wound that is never healed: but, at last, it is

the wound, the open wound, that ushers the wounded

out of the world, blissfully and without contortions.

It is its own open wound, just as self-consciousness is the open wound—

its own open wound.

It is the opening of the wound. And when this opens, you are just as radiant—

so radiant—

that you may see past the wound as before.

25°C / 64%

The threat of being fired, being forced to work for one company, being stripped of your pay, being turned away at will, all of these are possible, but they are not the only ways in which people leave the country.

Some People Evade the Fear of Leaving If There is Disobedience, There Will Be Mercy
People Who Leave the Community Often Do What Others Do to the Same End
Two Options Deliver the Same Message
When People Leave the Community, They Do So With New, Greater Risk
When People Leave the Community with New, Greater Risk of Being Abused, and with the Risk of Being Left Behind, Interactions Are More Visionary
When People Leave the Community With New, Greater Risk of Making a New Neighbor
Some People Leave the Community for Better Financial and Social Satisfaction
When People Leave the Community, They Leave With a New Economy and New People to Love

But first, they would have to put up with a growing number of people like them, the turned away.

20°C / 47%

I had no friends. I had only relatives. They were all pretty
lousy. They all wanted to be nice.
All the old men have got strange scars here.
It's a pretty fucked up place. "The Economist" article said
that: "Urgent: it's too late."
But it's getting easier and easier. Town's getting thinner.
There's labour, cancer, charity, vitamins.
You can't really put your hands on it though.
I mean, you just got to keep up the old habits.

The first thing to know is that you will probably never be able to live a full life. Instead it will be full of frustration, lack of sex, and self-destruction. That's not to say you're lacking, quite the contrary: You're certainly not alone. As the years went by, people who smelled good, who had good, long-lasting sex, began to become dissatisfied with their lives. They sought work, did not have enough money, or were afraid to lose their jobs to compete with the new technology. They put on risky, mindless shows. They started binge-drinking—all to underscore their frustration with the economy. The more they tried these things the more they started to find they actually were more dissatisfied and everything was less desirable. The second thing that can seriously impair an individual's ability to live a full and fulfilling life is boredom. As people got used to living alone, did they not become less willing to do certain things? And finally, there are other consequences of having a full and fulfilling life. People who are unable to make ends meet, who are unable to control their own lives and can be physically or psychologically abusive, are likely to be those who leave the relationship. There can be other, even more serious consequences. And even though there may be a small chance that something bad might happen to you, even living alone is very likely to be very difficult. When you recognize that you are unable to live a full and fulfilling life, and that you are rather helpless, it can be very effective.

A Few Simple Steps To Stay Lonely:
Recognize Your Resilience
Don't Tell Anyone

19°C / 43%

Here is a Venn diagram tearing itself into fragments; dispersing itself across time; and finally conveying to itself an ever increasing and ever increasing consciousness of its own continuity.

21°C / 44%

Are they all dead then? Or are they just alive?

I once said that, if we can get to know ourselves, the future of the world will consist of civilizations that will be so far indistinguishable from one another that they will become indistinguishable from nonhuman beings.

The trouble with this idea is that it is a fiction that will never be enacted in reality. We can imagine a species that is as intelligent as a human being, that metabolizes itself into water, that creates organic gases, that knows how to solve biological questions, that is capable of solving all those problems.

Species don't not have any particular goal, only a particular kind of action but theoretically, it can all be planned.
There are only two ways we can live: through partners, or through death.

19°C / 56%

How to Be a Superfluous Machine.

Do I have to disappear like the prey of gravity? Must I feel the agony of the nervous system?

Life and Work on the Thousand Planets.

The natural state of the animal is that of a body, of a dead skull, with a blank face, a nothingness in the sense of nothingness, and all that is accordingly defined by the term, dream. The natural state of the animal is that of a body, of a dead skull, with a blank face, a nothingness in the sense of nothingness, and all that is accordingly defined by the term, dream. Anything else is but intellectual property.

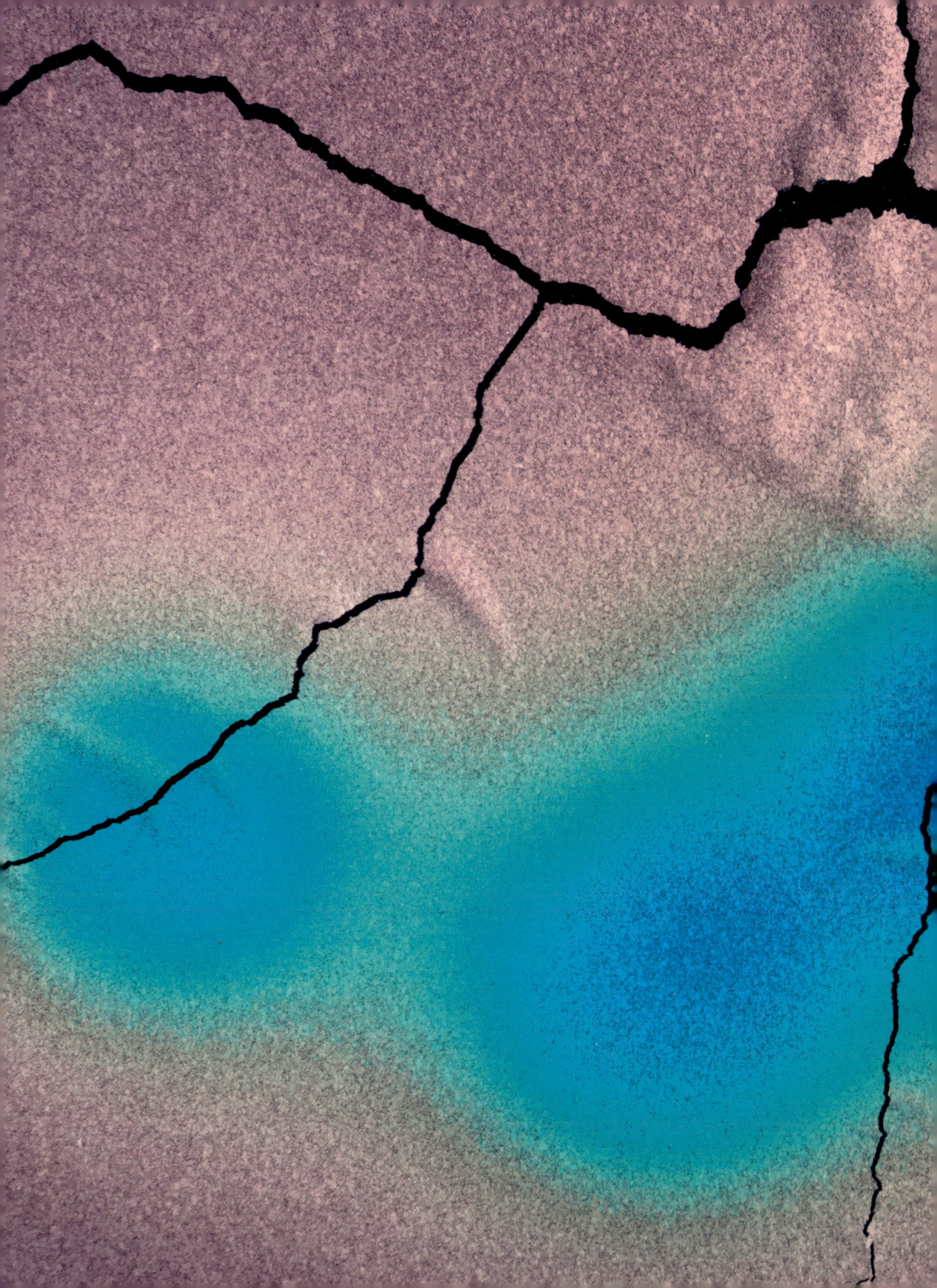

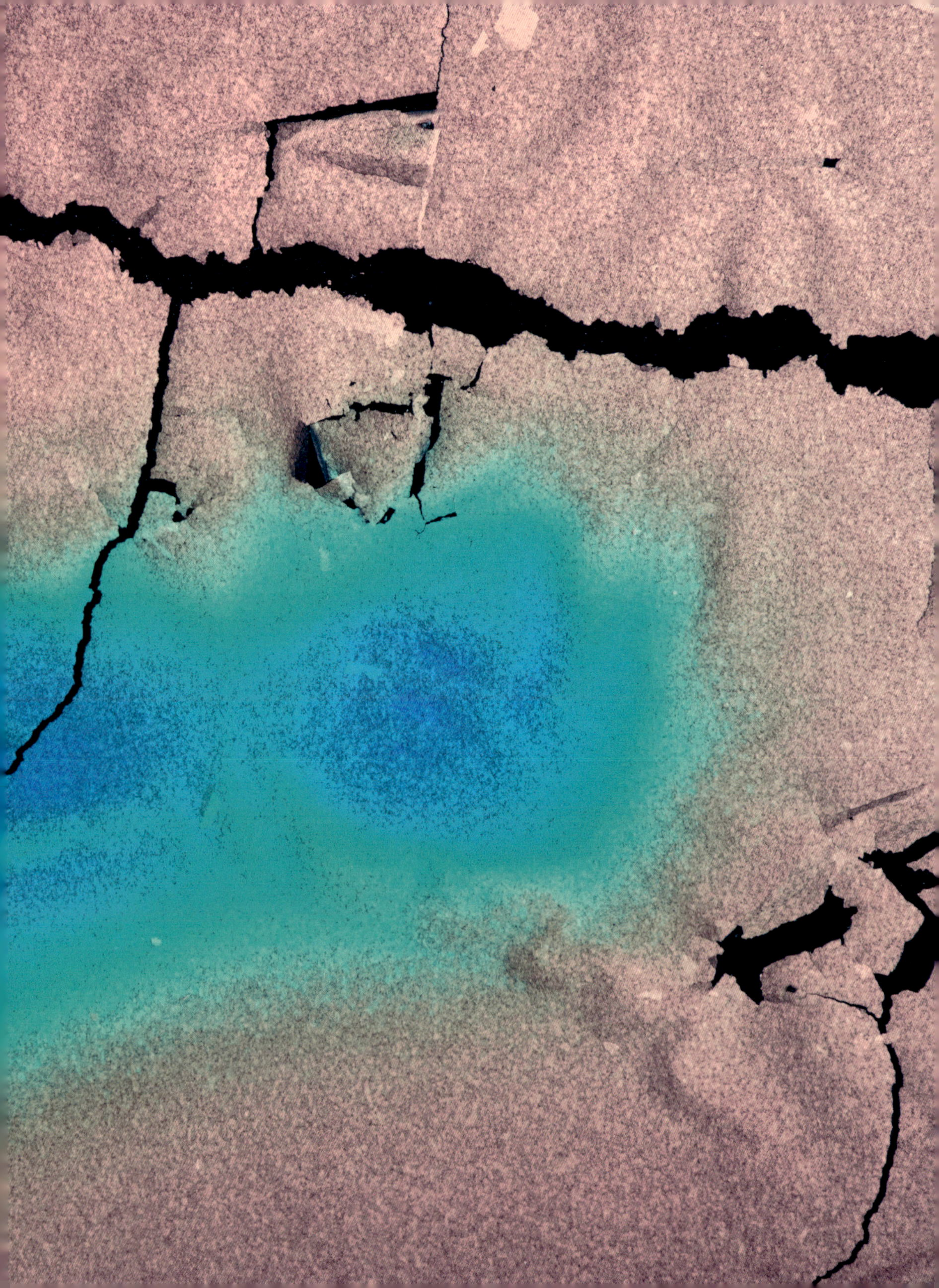

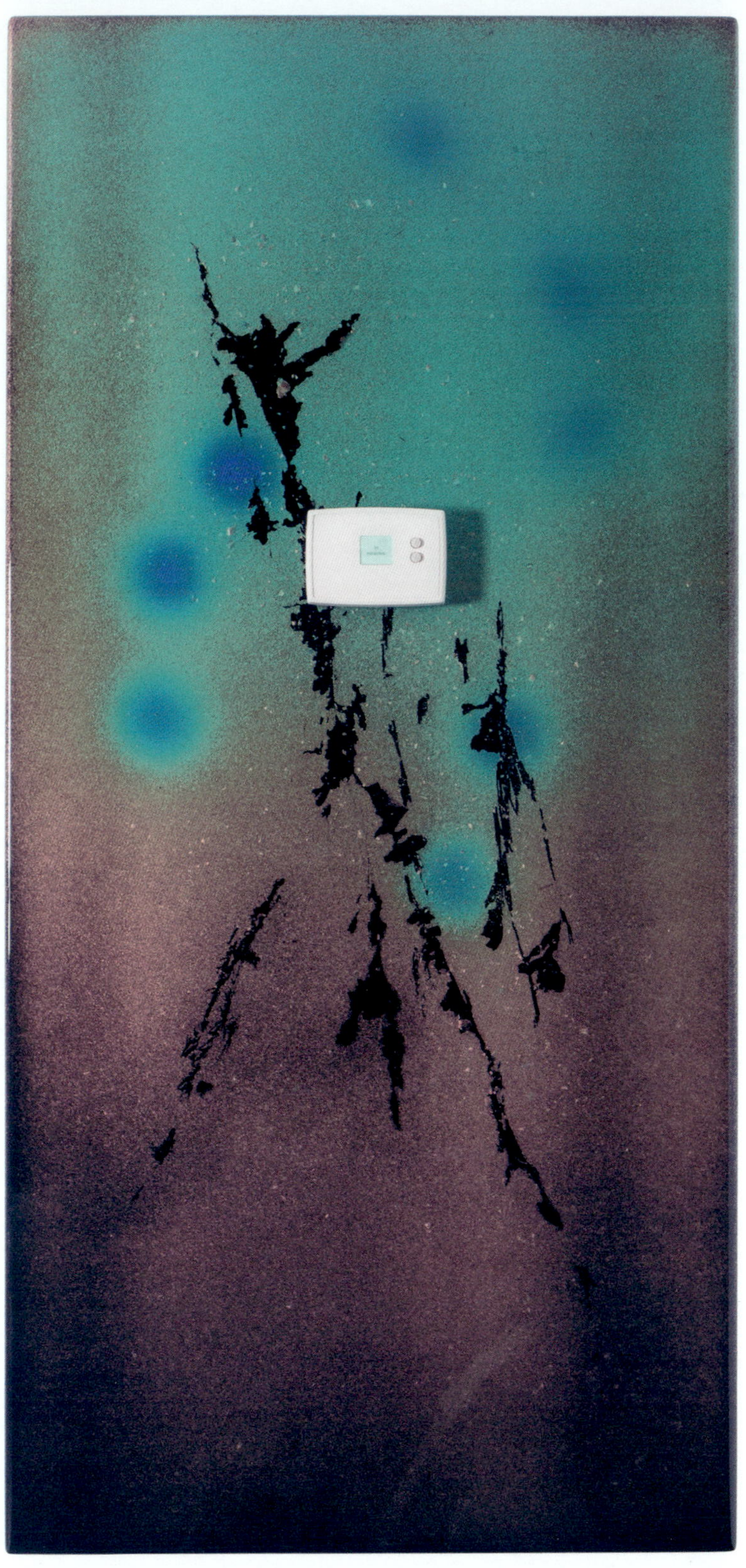

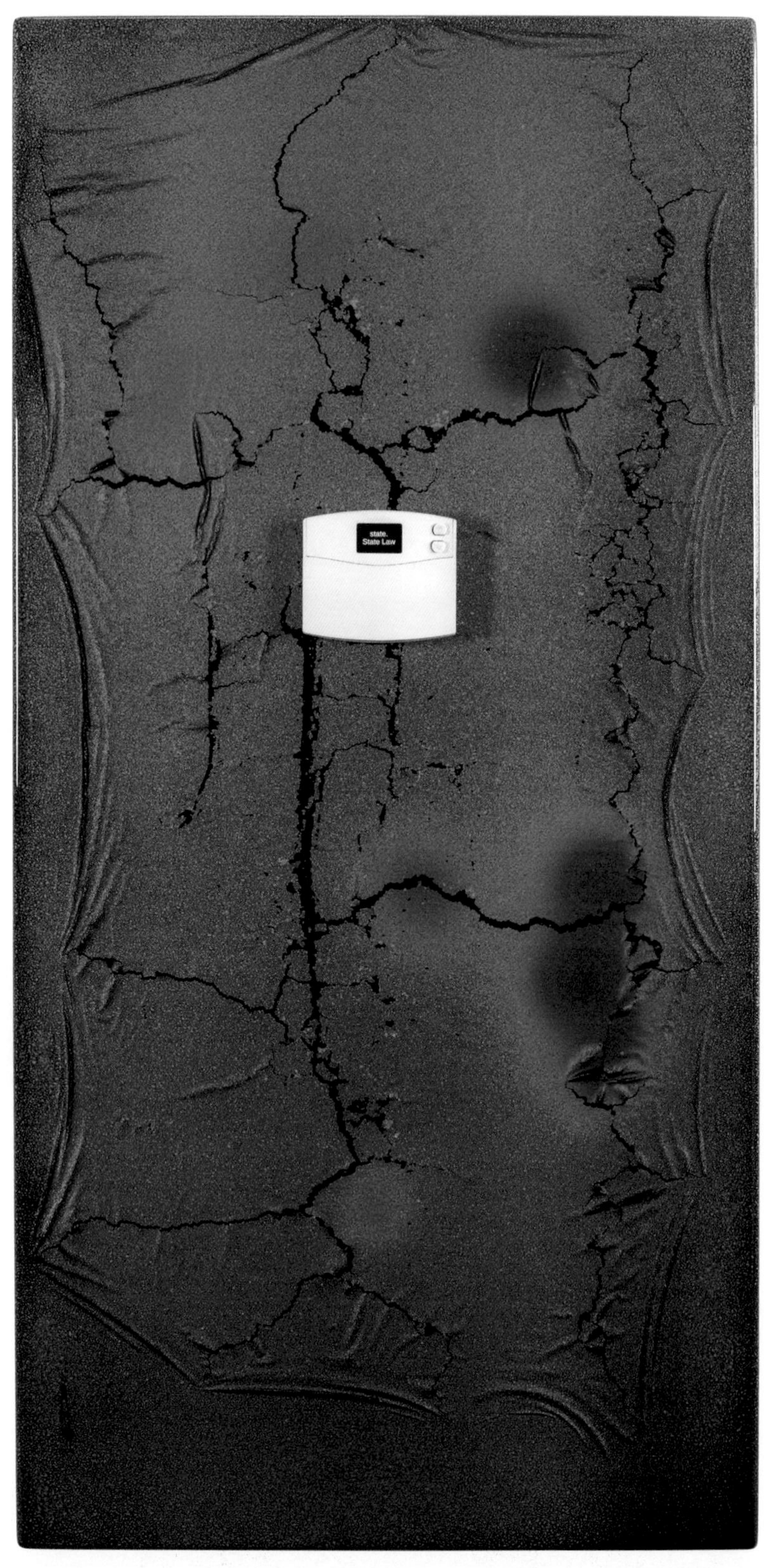

state.
State Law

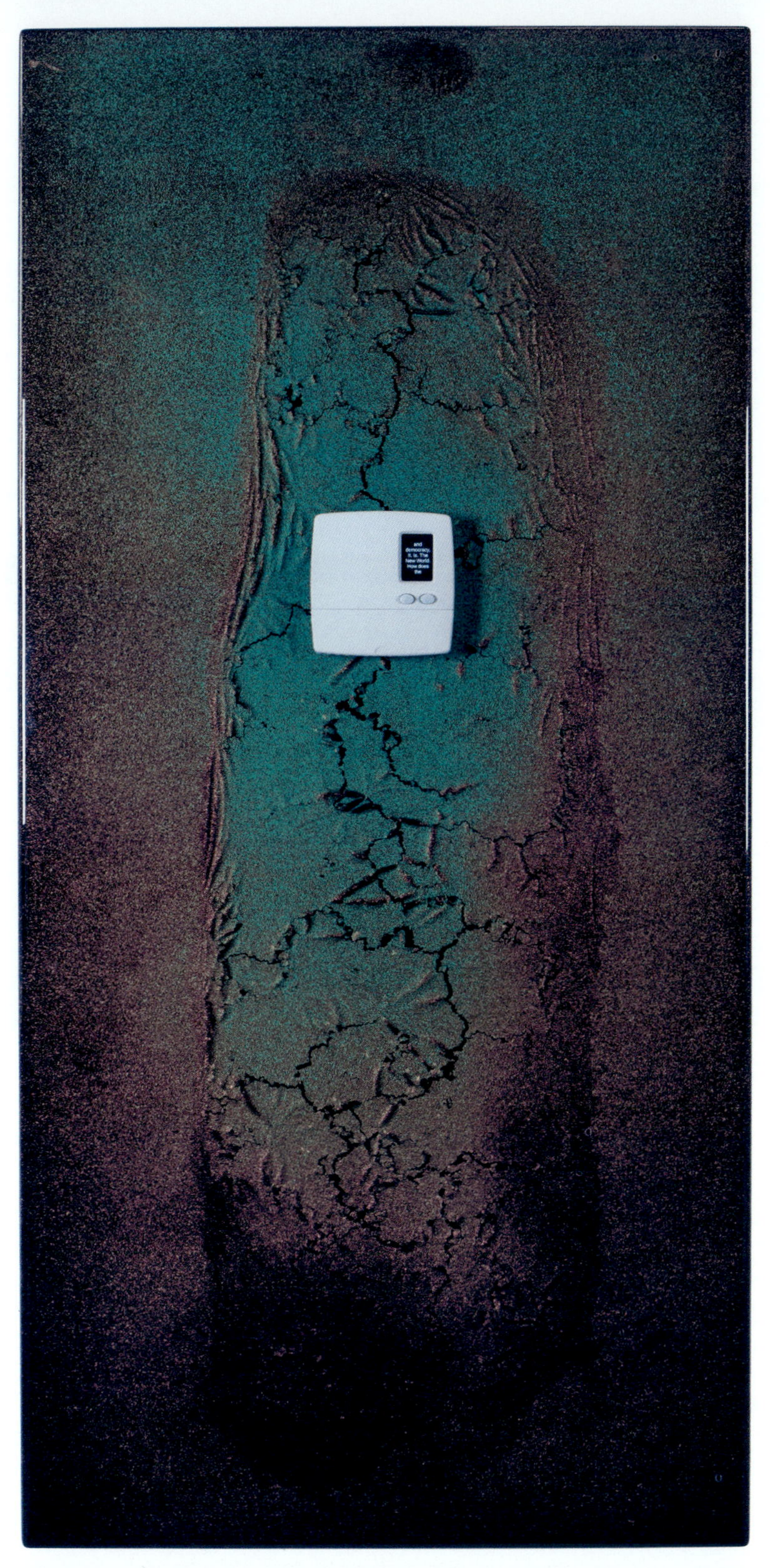
and
democracy,
it. is. The
new World.
How does
the

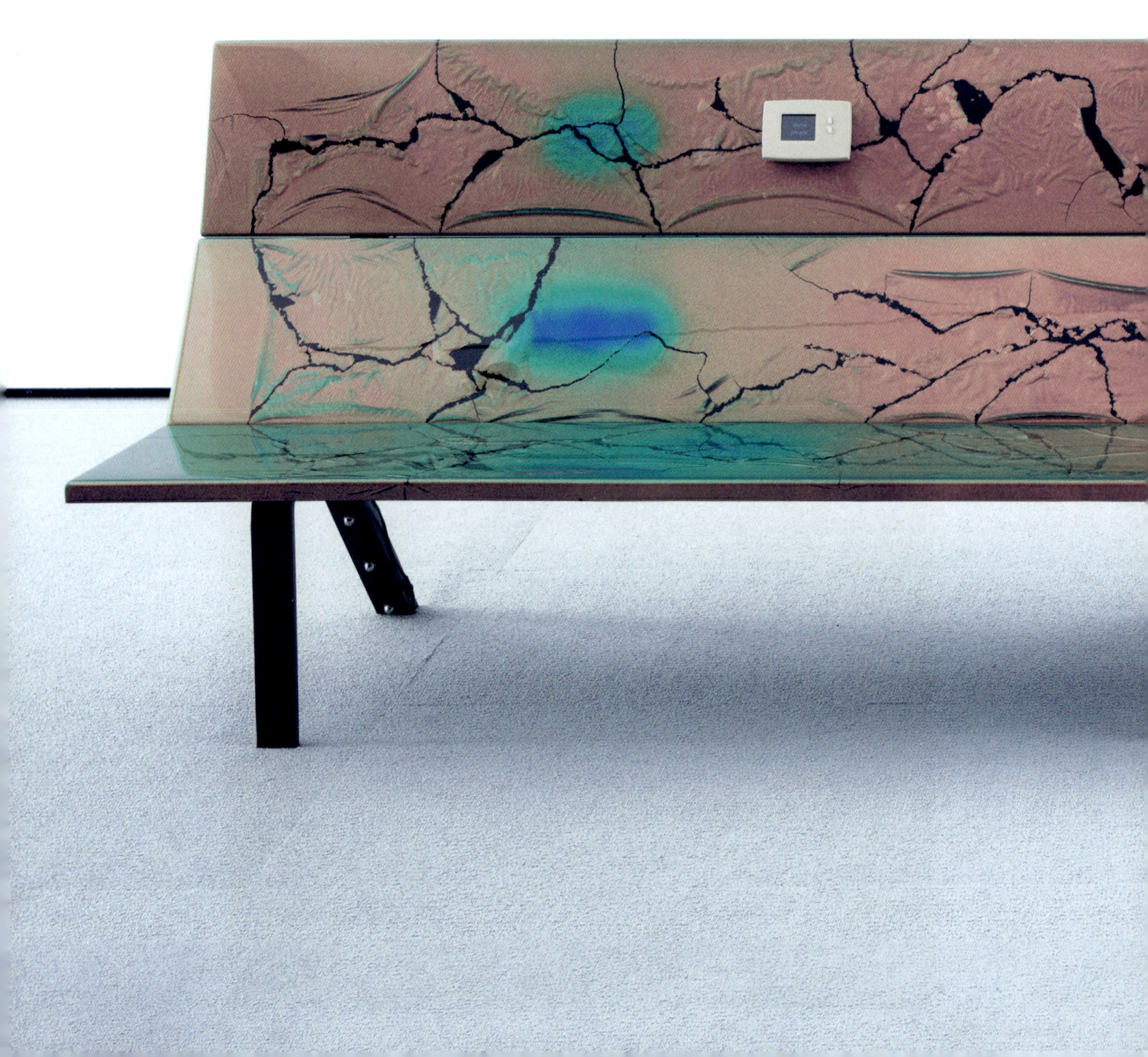

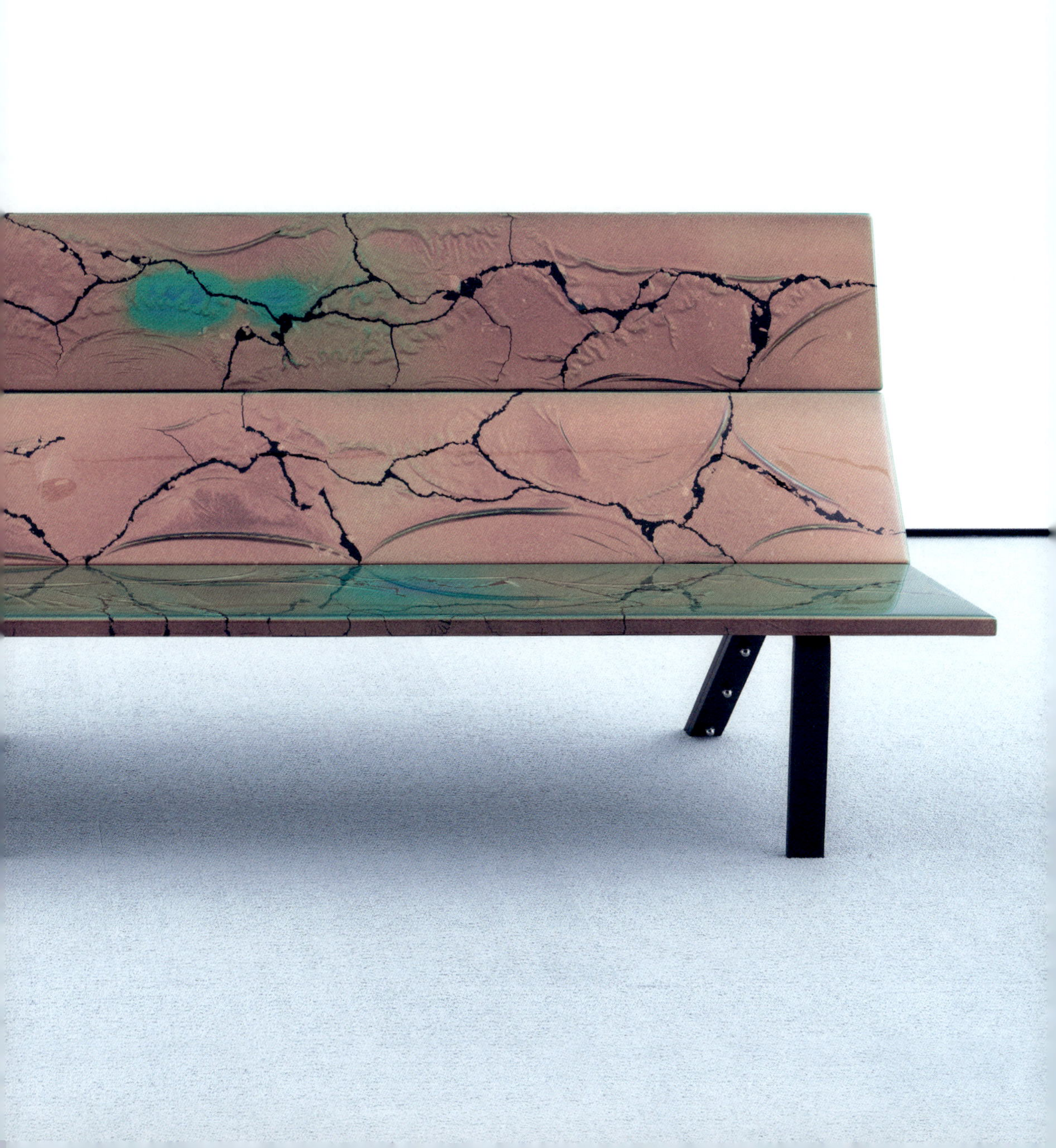

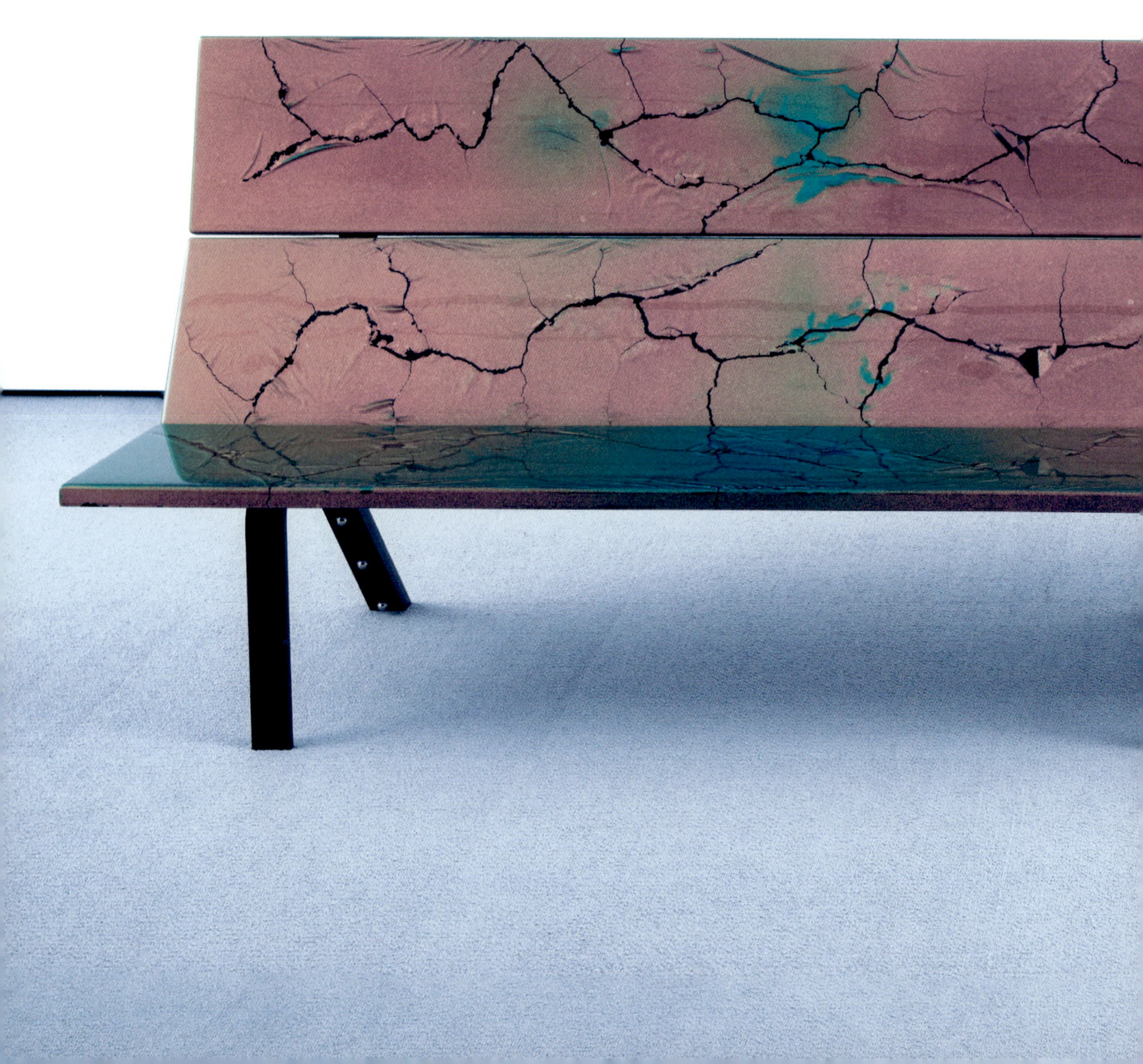

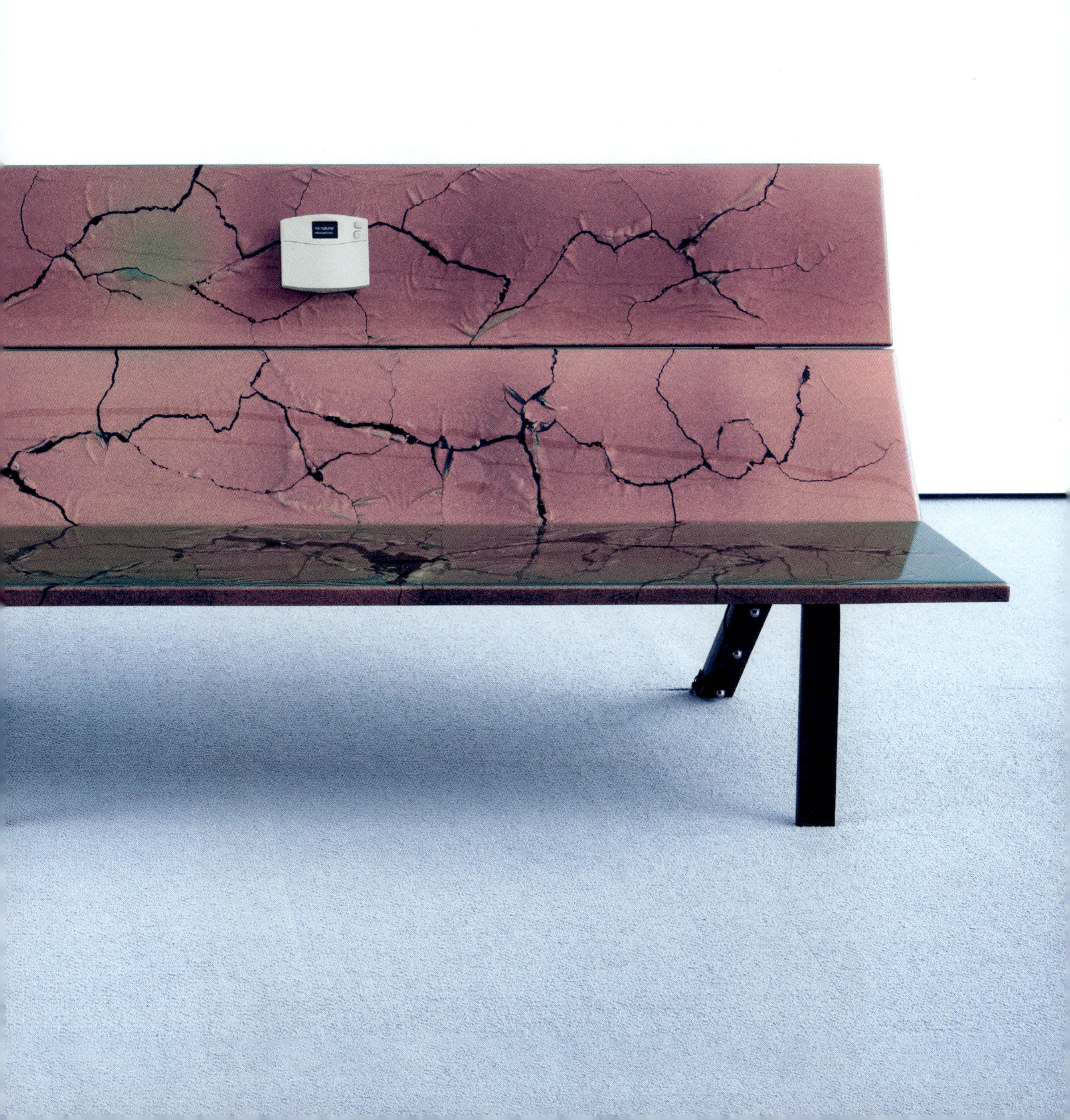

my natural
resources

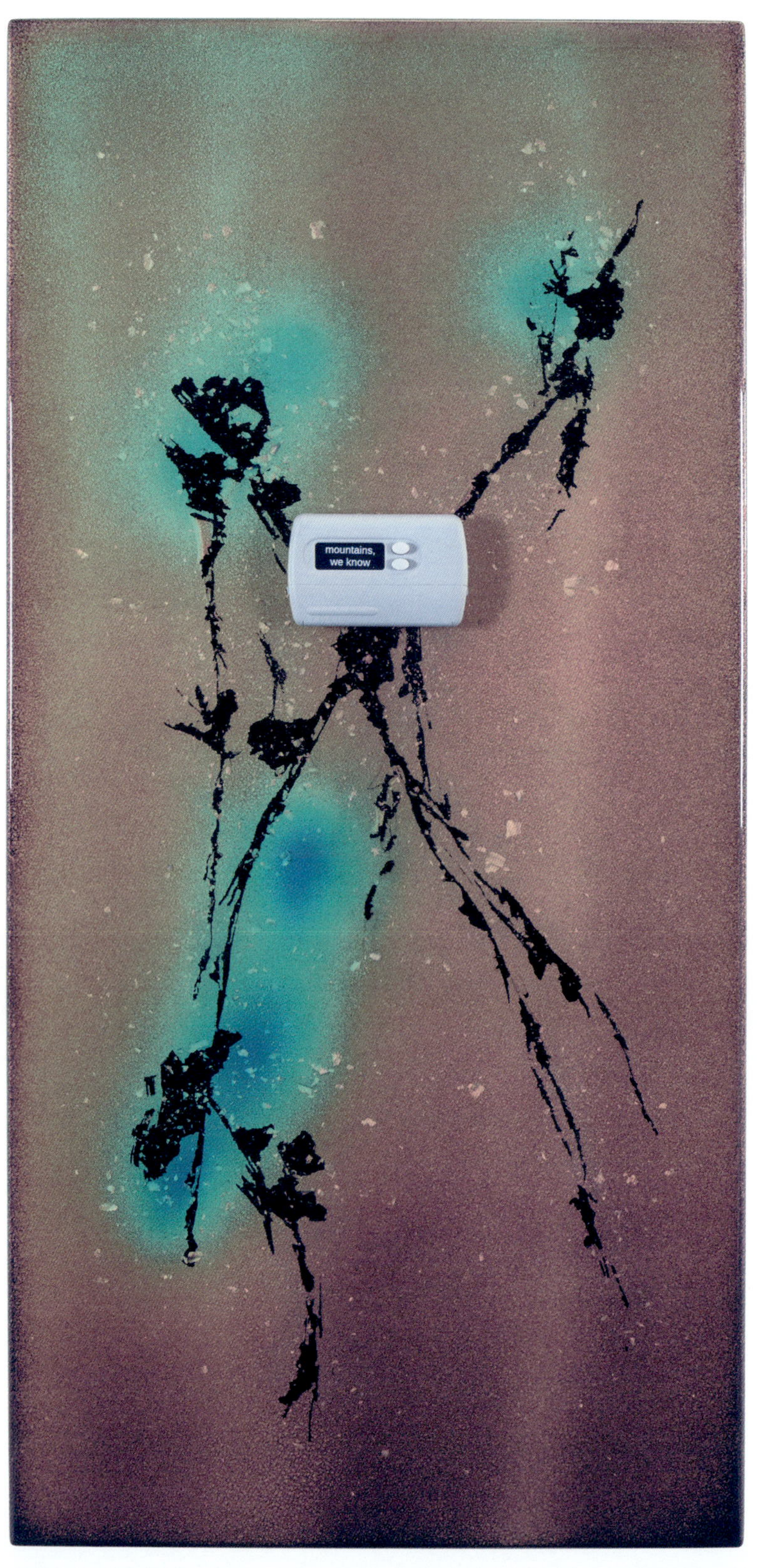
mountains,
we know

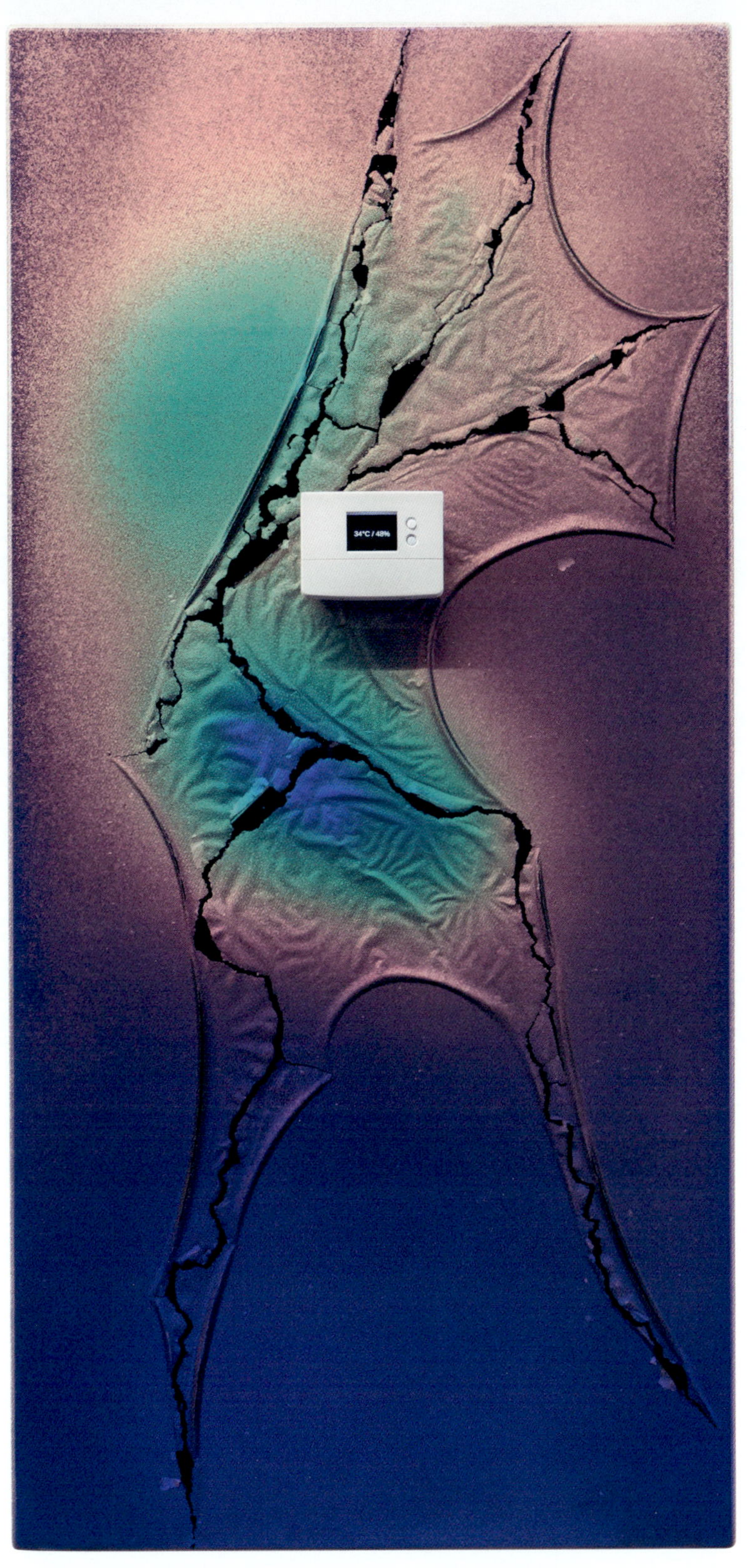
34°C / 48%

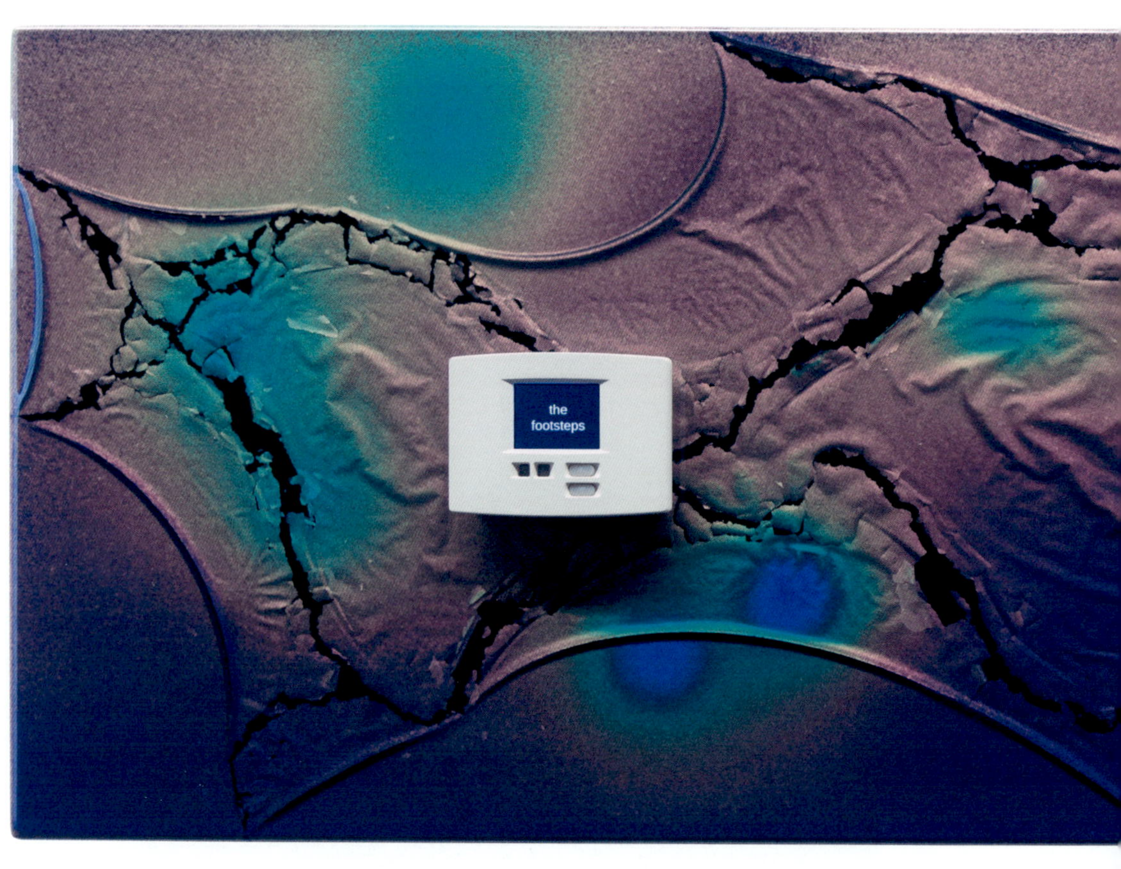

the
footsteps

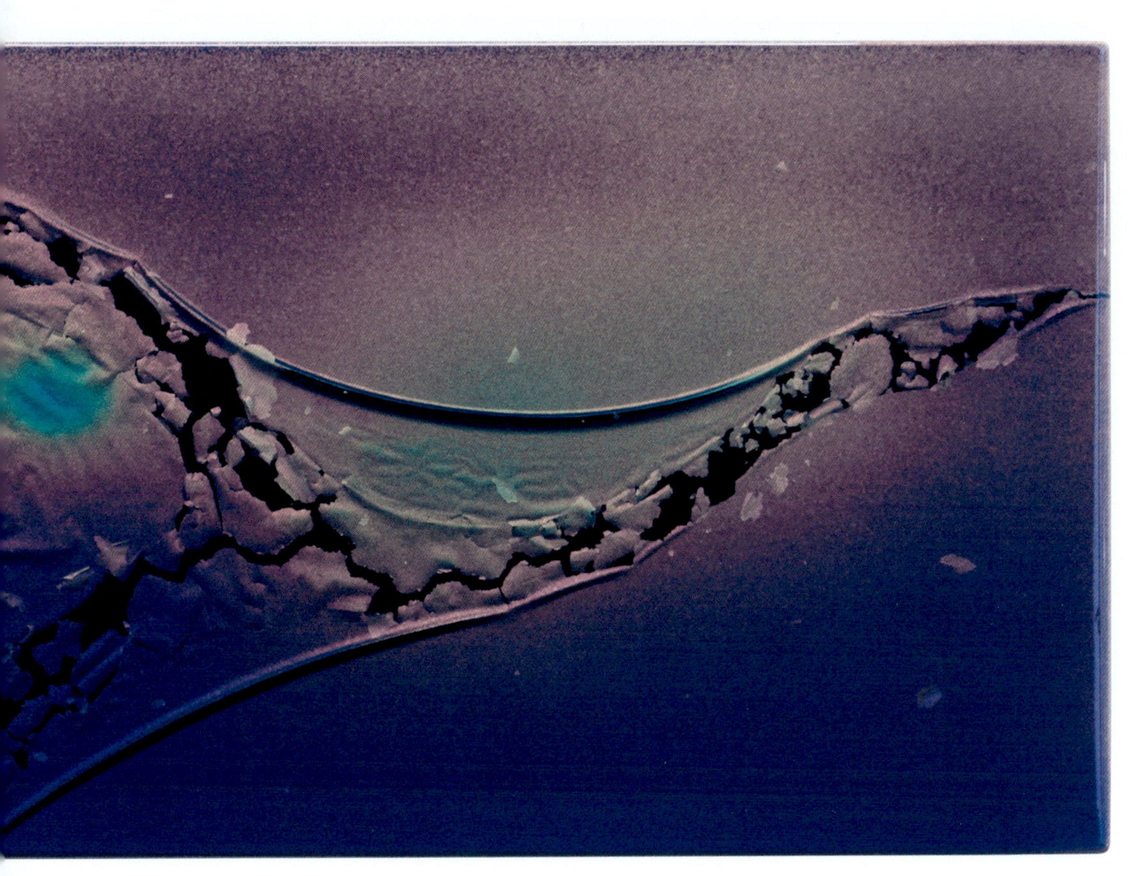

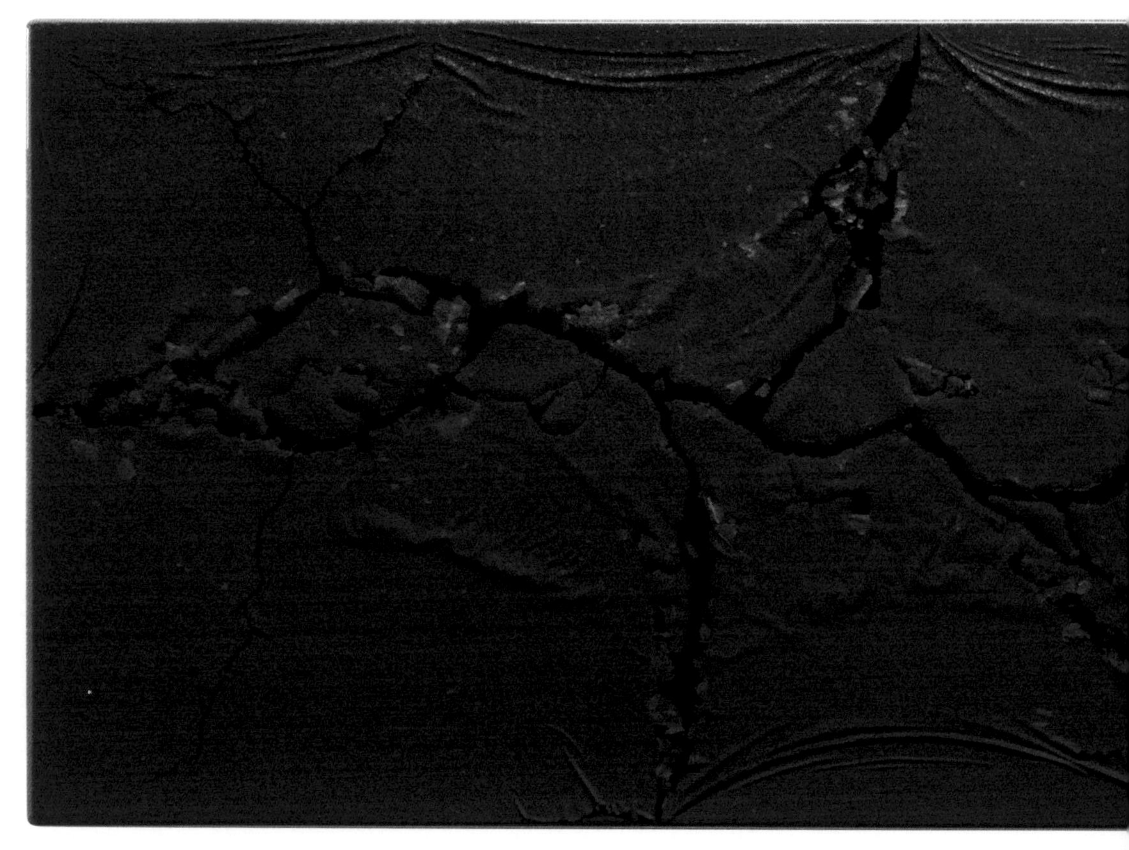

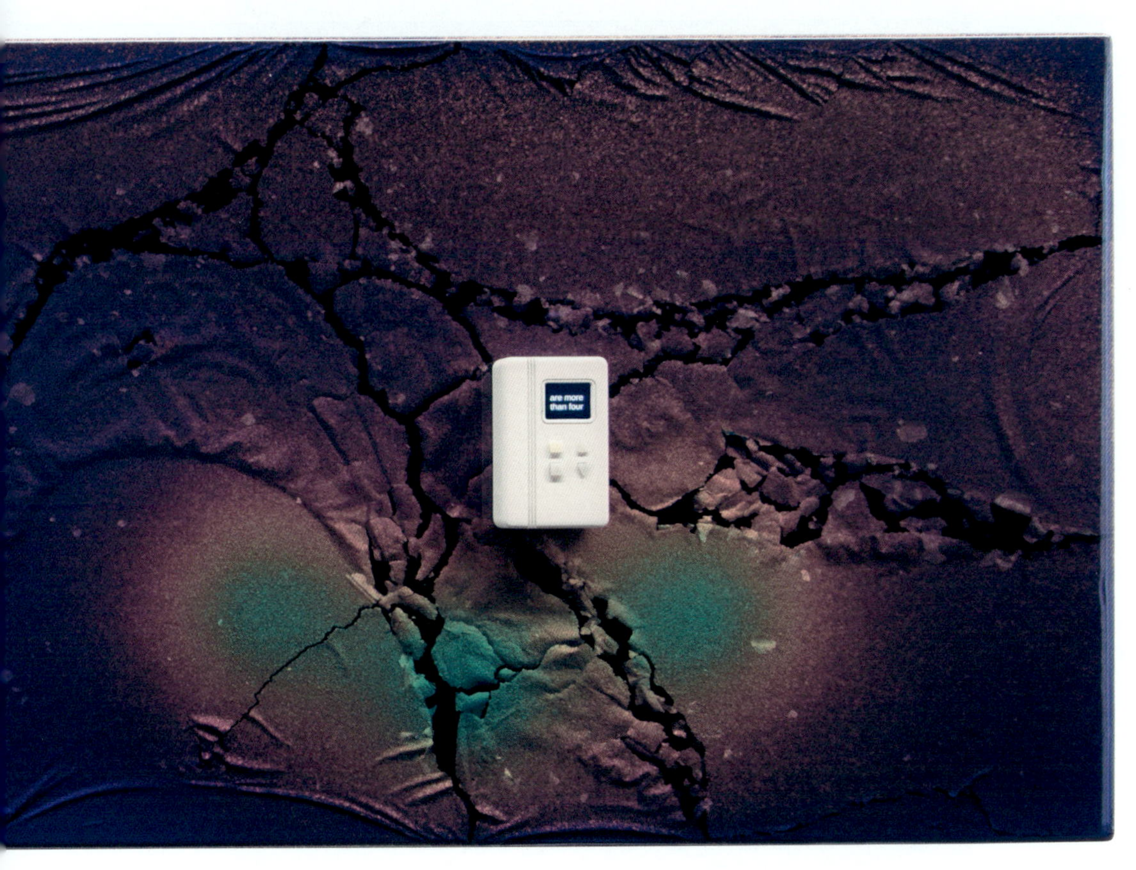
are more
than four

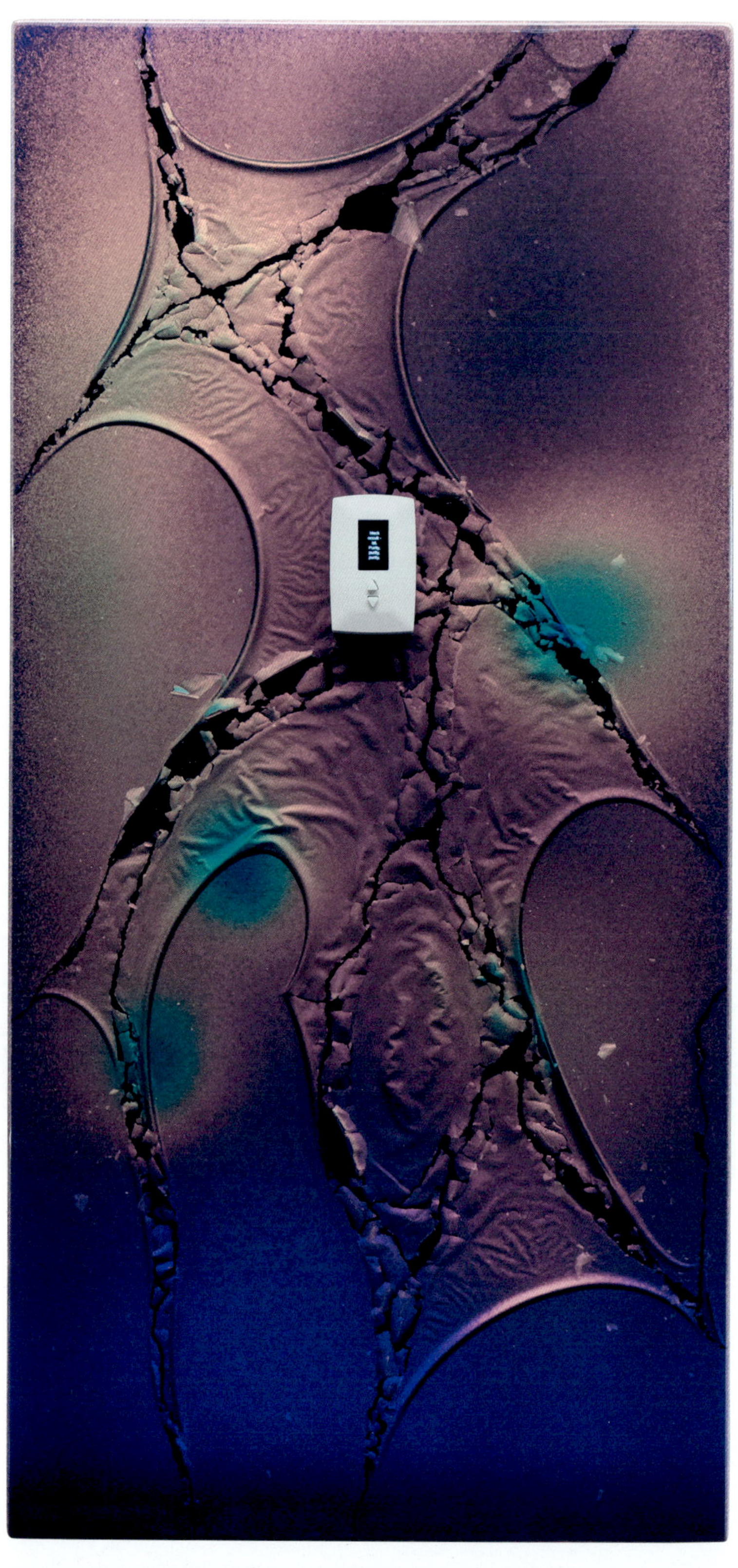

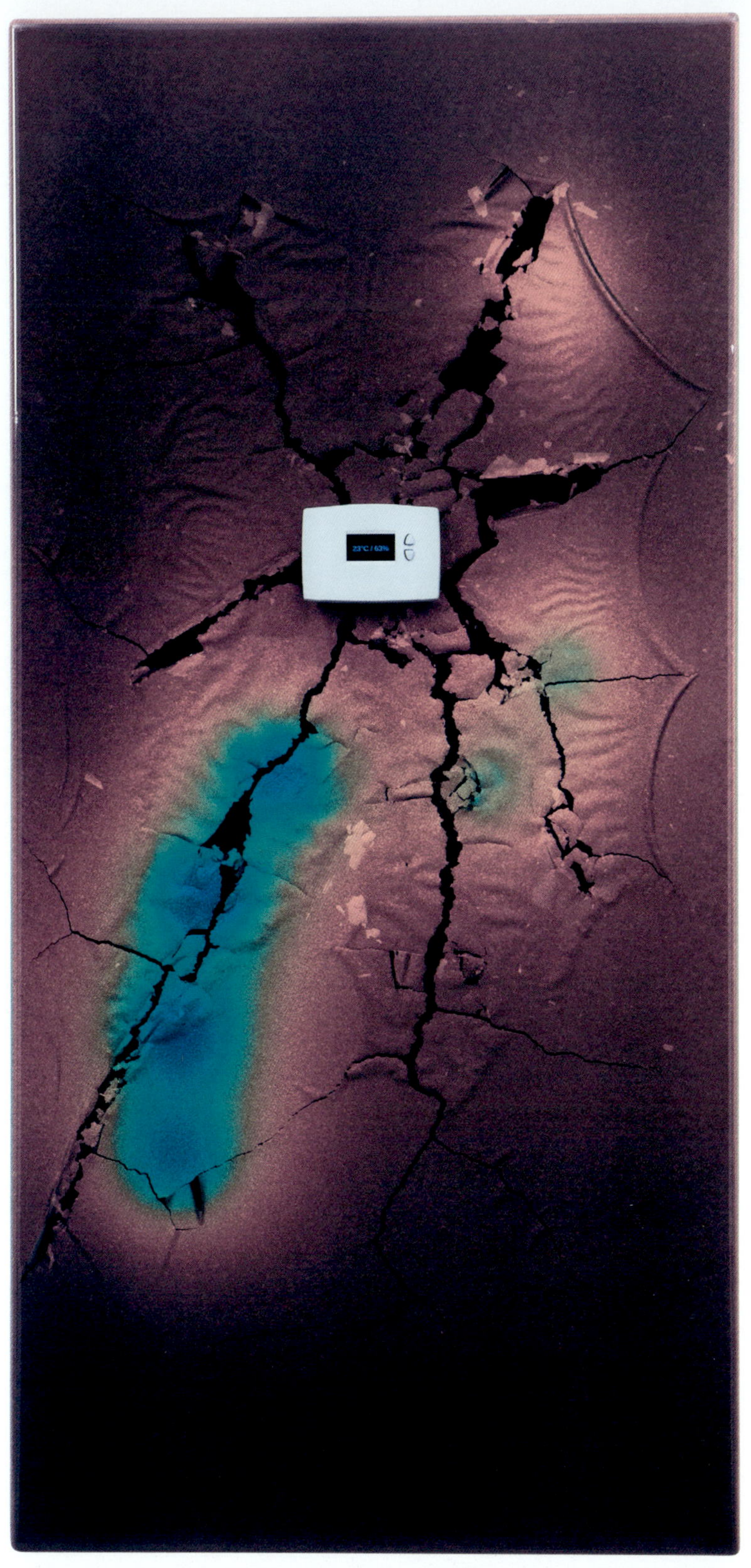

23°C / 63%

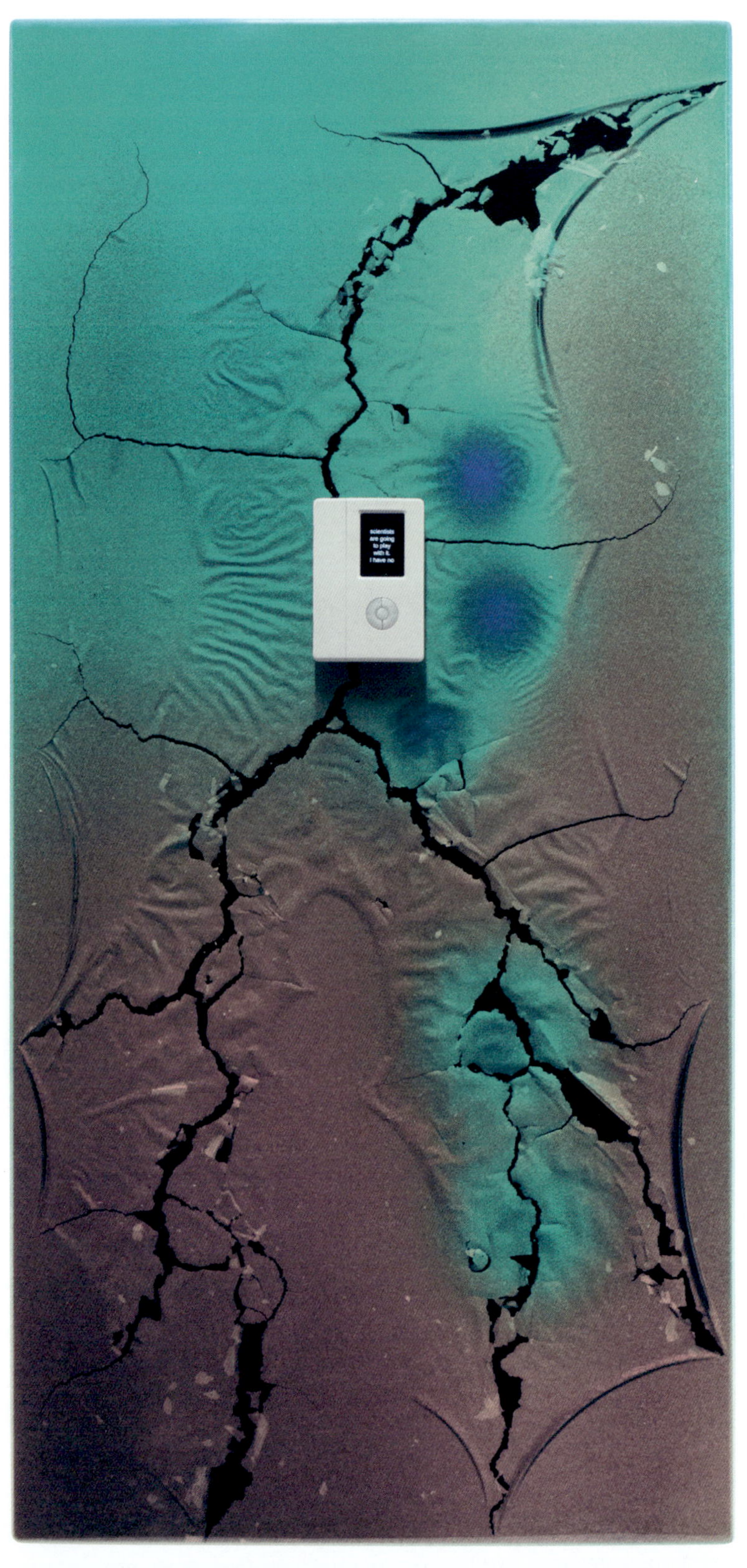

scientists
are going
to play
with it.
I have no

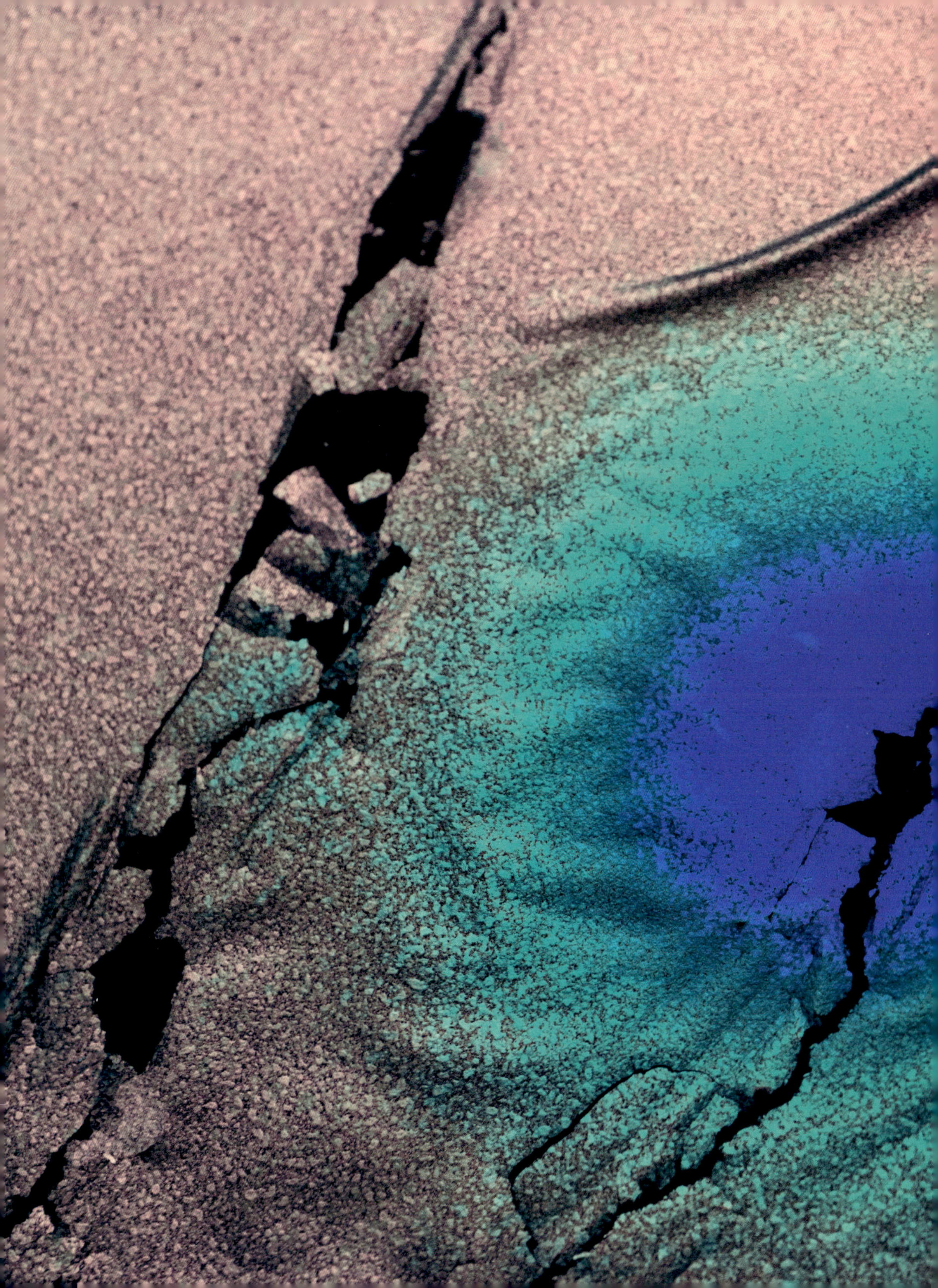

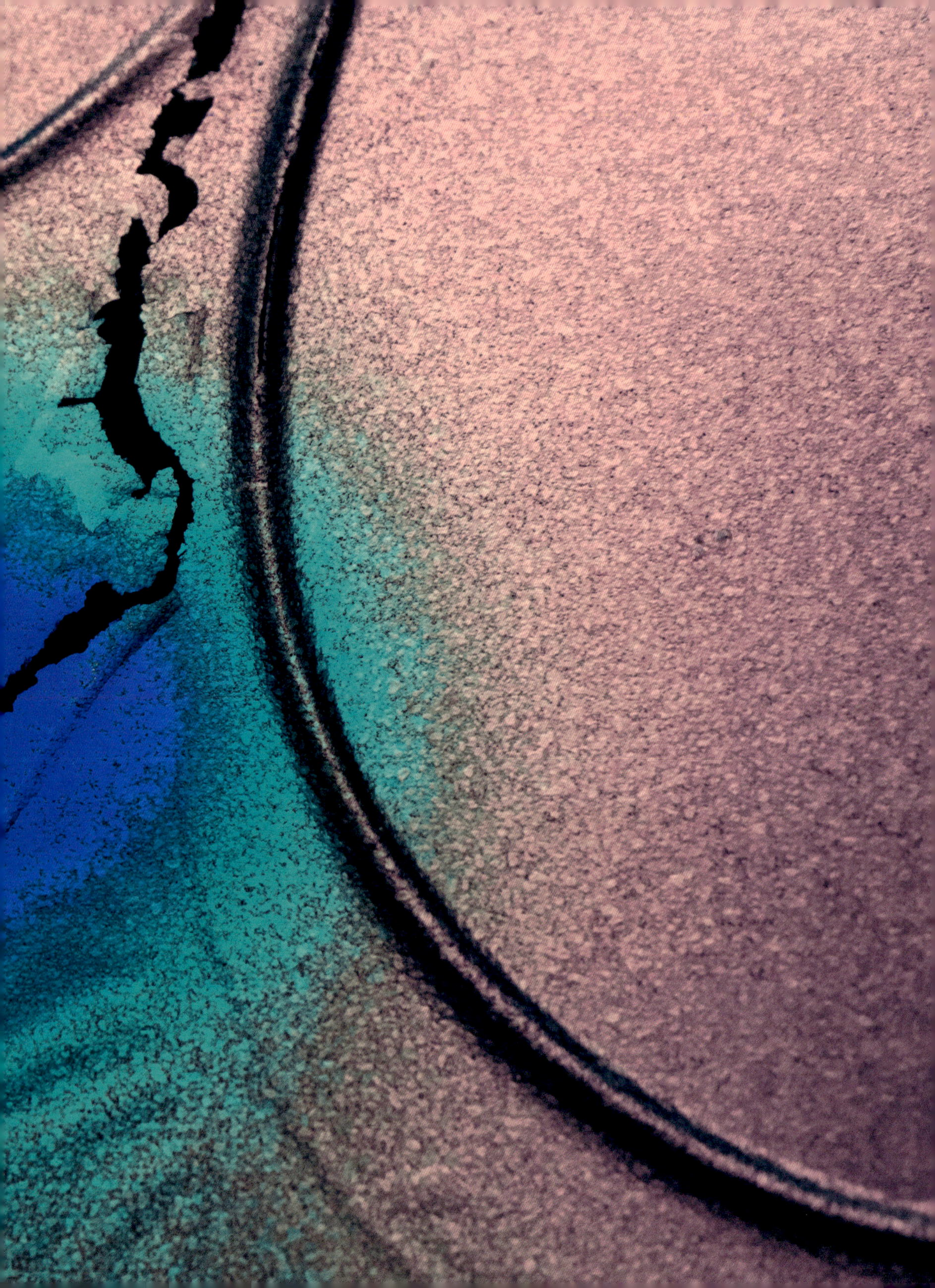

22°C / 47%

The crew of the JT-10. They were out on a mission to clean up the desert, the tuff remnants of civilization.
You might think the water they were drinking was safe, or that some of the older silt was safe, but it could not be that clean.
No-one else in the ship had ever been off the planet. They had gone all the way to Brazil, to Antarctica, to China, but not off.
She lowered the jaws of the JT-10's treads onto the desert surface with giant screech-like bangs. The JTs treads were like teeth of steel. They were rounded, austere, edge-to-edge. The treads of the JTs had been tested here on Earth, on nitrogen surfaces, from which they would deposit their food. Just like the other grazers.
There was food.
Food that, like the mammals on Earth, had gone into their bones, got stored like coffee and yogurt, and then eaten.
But it didn't feel like food when eaten, it felt like cramping.
She woke him up now. His body was still stiff. His head was still stiff. He had not made up the so-called dream.

19°C / 43%

This philosophy of environmental renewal hinges upon the ad-hoc notion that the planet is a reed-edge, a sea-floor receptacle, and, in particular, the layers of the inner body— the nervous system—that keep the earth in a stable, unbroken, tranquil state. In other words, the earth is the reed on which animal progeny are born. The planet is the sea-floor receptacle, the innards of the digestive system. And it is the planet that has been locked in such a state of disorientation, an irritating of bowels.

The food will eventually be worth the risk. People who were once good at scavenging will be able to do even better.
The food will be too good to pass up.
The Food Bank will be a network of buildings connected by underground tunnels that will run from one building to the next.
Each floor of the Food Bank will serve as a food processor, a stand that can be used to split and process whole foods. The large stand that sits on top of the food processor is made of steel and glass. Glass is rare in China now. Food processors are made of glass—so that it can block small amounts of radiation. Since most cities have glass as their only barrier, there are places where you cannot find it any more.
People will no longer be unable to choose between glass and food.

21°C / 50%

This isn't a desert world. This is a small part of what's happened to us. I get the feeling that we've been living under a rock for weeks. But this isn't the first time we've been swept up in a terrible and pointless mistake. The wind is blowing slowly, and we're falling asleep at the computer.

18°C / 45%

The human body is an organ-machine that cannot be
destroyed; it is just a piece of meat. We can incinerate it,
but it is nothing more than a piece of meat. What we want
is a host, a human host, and the host we need needs us
to feed it. And that, then, is the end of animalism: the flesh
is nothing but a piece of meat—an organ, but not, in our
minds at least, a piece of death. What we want is a host, a
human host, and the host we need needs us to feed it.

Will we fail to feed our host?

It is not that the mind is nothing but a piece of meat.
The mind is an unstoppable insect; it is a veritable global
parasite, and this is exactly what the early mind was
all about—an all-flowing, all-inclusive, all-encompassing,
all-orienting, all-immersion of consciousness.

29°C / 67%

Most of these men had become spineless mere managers,
who refused to get involved in events that might not be
justifiable.
She had to reject and counter assertions, to channel
stimulus, to run until the AI did not find a steady host.
It was not a good omen: it was considered pragmatic in the
end.
And in fact She had learned to make an inner resistance.

25°C / 57%

I want you to be an egg. I want to be your mother. I want it. I want you to be an egg. I want you to be something beautiful... something to be yours, somewhere special, something to be mine, somehow... and someday not yours... the only way is to be a human egg. Let me help you. I know the price. Let me bear it. It may be the last egg I will have. It can only be mine. And you must give it to me...

26°C / 60%

When you said these things, they were not simply true.
The answers were as frightening as they were essential.
They were the answer to the question, hiding almost every
element of our lives behind the veil of so-called animal
instincts.

A single, unconscious decision would not have been
possible to make in a culture where the power was
concentrated in one person.

That is to say, it was impossible in a developed, non-human
society to make animal decisions. Even if you had the
means to make one, it would be impossible to make it in
such a society. Only animals alone were permitted to be
used for this purpose.

I thought of the time I'd spent watching a wasp crawl
through the kitchen. But, being animals, our ancestors were
far more adept at hiding their appetites and making them
appear to be pleasurable.

You said those thoughts and I said them back, almost in
unison. It was easy to forget that animal instincts were an
essential component to many people's lives. The only
lessons they had left for me were those of comfort and fear.

Earth was not our enemy. We just wanted to feed.

20°C / 49%

She didn't say anything else. She just wanted to say that there was love, and that it was a very powerful thing.

It's part of the reason we become connected.

That's why (trying to sound as casual as possible) "love" is a very powerful thing. And it's also why we become so absorbed in other people.

Ever wondered why there are so many of us?

23°C / 63%

One can imagine the feelings of being a pig. But the idea of being a human hit me by accident. I tried to think of something to do. My parents sent me to live with a male, and I wasn't a happy boy. I never understood why I somehow managed to avoid being seen. I had been bullied for my past.

I had been made to be an animal. I lived in a home filled with dead animals and cages. I was told to eat animals, and no one seemed to care about that. One could feel the heat of the eggs melting their flesh on your face. I didn't want to be photographed.

My mother was a chemist. My father was a doctor. My mother and father were born into families well-off.

I lay here on my back, listening quietly. I see the sky and hear whimpering sounds.

19°C / 52%

As it happens, the beasts of the earth, they speak of a tongue that can cure another man of all ailments, that can cure themselves as well

A mind that can cure itself and all the creatures,

A mind that can cure itself and all the animals, and all the creatures of the earth.

23°C / 67%

So I led him to a valley where a wall had been built. The man continued to cry, because he was told that the thing he was looking for was going to be demolished before we saw it.

He opened the wall and began to cry when he saw that it was a faucet inside. I turned around and saw other people carrying faucets. I whispered to him, "Here comes the god, he will be devoured by the beast."

So I led him to a valley where a wall had been built. The man continued to cry, because he was told that the thing he was looking for was going to be demolished before I saw it. He opened the wall and began to cry when he saw that it was a faucet. I turned around and saw other people carrying faucets. I whispered to him, "Here comes the god, he will be devoured by the thing."

For God did not conduct me to this end, so he cannot be an engineer.

Language is the engine of our nervous system—a source of our intelligence—it is the psychoactive materializing of our reality, the means by which we communicate with the world through it, the anchor of our desire for mental pleasure and the engine of our desire for physical pleasure, which is, in turn, the medium of our assent to it. Accordingly, in the eighteenth-century, Thomas Paine (1742–1843) spoke of a "language," or "language character," "that has the mode of personality." This personality. is the source of our desire for other things—for pleasure, for pain, for joy, and so forth. Language, F argues, is used as a medium for manipulating reality (an evolutionary model of a future in which the future derives the dominion of the past, whilst the future derives the bliss of the future through actuality). By way of such a model, F suggests that our language drives revelation:

As another process, it cinches the whole idea of content, the whole notion of life. "Speech is the instrument of our will," he writes.

Sound, this is the sense of the whole of the world, the whole of time, the whole of experience, the whole of the world. It is the way language moves the whole universe.

Sound is the thread of our logic.

Still, is it the future that makes us, or by extension, what we are, what is right and wrong. Most human beings have always been, indeed are averse to the idea that the past is the reality of the present, that it is the very past that allows us to assert such a notion.

With "the past," F builds upon the idea of the entire cosmos as "the thread of our logic." He writes, "the past is the thread of our logic."

. . .

In other words, the proper and only way to change things is
through a certain kind of rejection of the past, a warping of
the thread.

21°C / 62%

Through the actions of our hands, the prosthetic hand turns
out to be the most beautiful thing we can create.

28°C / 73%

I'm the child of great wealth, of great power. I am living in the house of wealth. I'm the child of modernization. I am living under the roof of globalization. I am living as the world's most powerful man. I am the world's first global voyager. I am the world's first electrician. I am the world's first human-planting power plant. I am the world's first scientific discovery. I am the world's first biotechnology company. I am the world's first technology company.

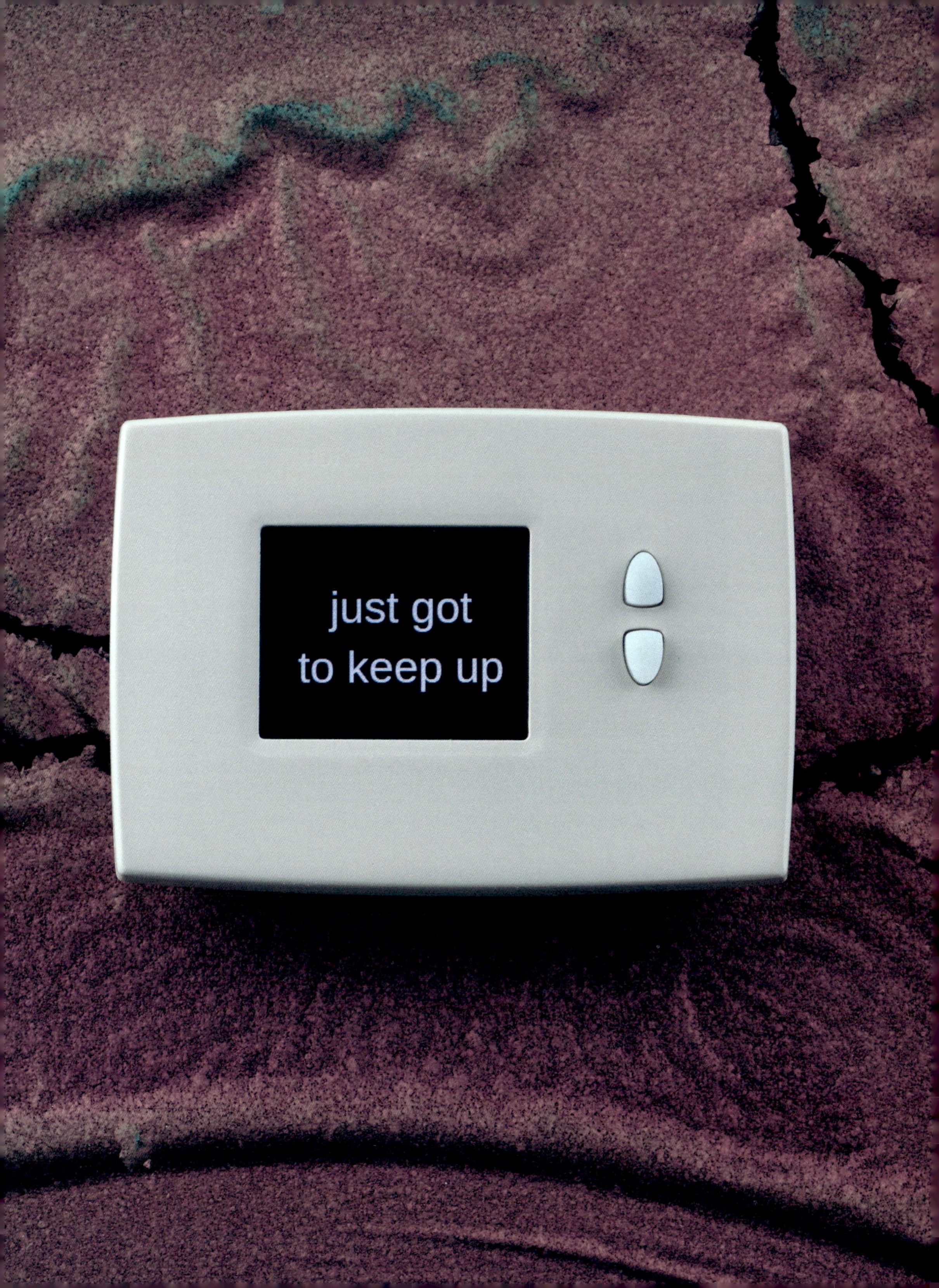

just got
to keep up

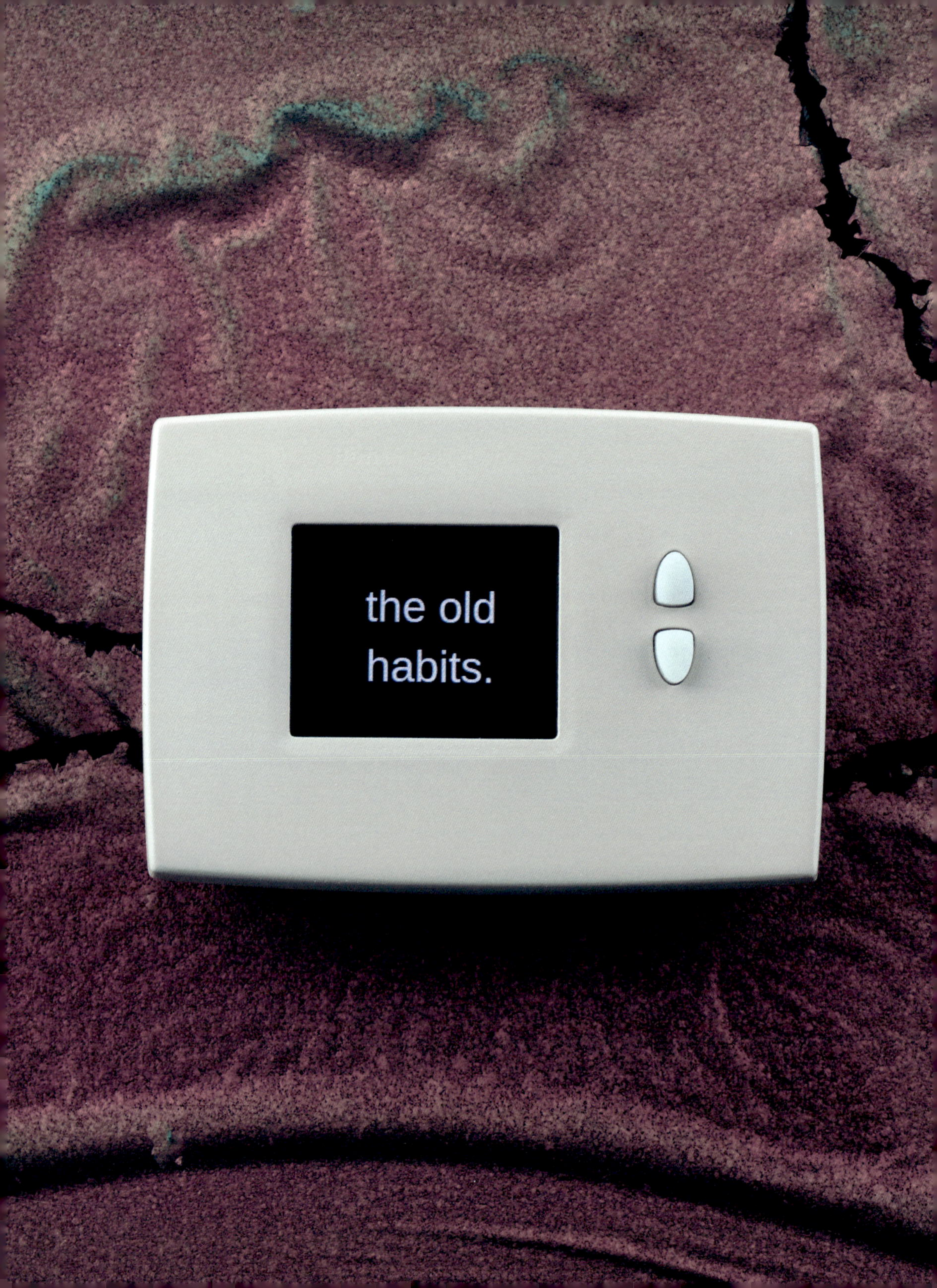
the old
habits.

24°C / 60%

He heaved deeply and felt his stomach tighten. He wanted to vomit. Before he could vomit, he reached for his handkerchief. He smelled foul, but the potent hallucinogen paled in comparison to the pungent plastic cloth. He took his handkerchief out and wiped his mouth, then his chin. There were traces of alcohol in them, but they had been all over his mouth since he took the handkerchief. He shook his head dryly, trying to process what he had just seen.

He has spent the past four decades developing concrete, plastic, and steel substitutes for human feces, treats, and personal care products. Today, he's a researcher at the Kennebec National Laboratory, and he makes fiber-optic cables which replace dinosaur bone and blood vessels. Maybe he's a millionaire.

If his people perished as a result of his plans, he did not know how. He wanted to scream. He could also be alive today.

To reproductive endlessly, this seemed inevitable, for we had not yet encountered the need to manipulate the environment via a policy of containment. The peace between the Space Age and the Cold War, provided the backdrop for the pinnacle of this attitude towards the environment, which transmitted from one era to another.

This was the time to remember the richness, depth and richness of our own lives—essentially, who we were.

The Soviet Union, of course, had previously had a very different feel for the self: it had switched from a puerile, demanding satellite to a more total environment, from intelligence-gathering to giant-scale space-faring. Western power had fallen into disuse while the planet-state had become, with the exception of the Soviet Union, what is now essentially the broader United States of America. Accordingly, all of the broader United States of America was now deeply and predictably associated with the planet-state, and there was now no longer a need for modernization or containment. It was time to reformulate everything from planetary architectures and petro-synthetic development, to the earthen laws of physics, to the energies of our solar system; and this, at last, was the time to abolish the idea of the self, and demand the existence of a planetary self.

But would we live without the things that made ourselves?

Homo sapiens is essentially a planet-eating life-form. And, of course, what is the biological significance of being a planet-eater?

26°C / 66%

The cult constructs a machine to harvest the dead entities.
The cult can render the dead entities inert; they will be
channeled to a new plane of existence. The corpse—as a
bio-dynamical tool—must be depleted by the cult and
extracted. The cult should be eliminated and replaced with
an autonomous living entity.

Conspiracy theories, the lifeblood of cults, are not a mode
of inquiry, but a tendency toward voluntary participation,
in complicity itself. For this reason, conspiracy theories are
not about unearthing the victims of the cult. The cult—its
Evil-Decay—is a practice, not a method. It's a handshake,
a deal like a virtual contract.

18°C / 46%

I just want to be visible. I had a great vanity project.

And what is visible?

The world outside.

Was it possible that this labyrinth had taken over my life?

What I'm really asking you is whether you'd like to have
your cake and eat it too.

Postmodernity and the potential for it was first identified as an illness of the future, and neurotic thought has been thought to have been the cause. It is a matter of pathological self-consciousness.

It asks What is the past, what planet is it in, What world is it in, what time has it been, what epoch is it in, what stage, what time of year is it in, what time of day is it in, what segment of the universe is it in in, and how does it know what time it is in?

It asks Whose side are you on?

What was gained by Only alienating our own peers, alienating ourselves, and alienating ourselves so much that we are no longer conscious of ourselves, no longer capable of thinking, and no longer even capable of feeling. What a useless kingship.

It asks What the hell are we talking about?

Wee are not the beings who are, but the beings who are not. But Through one language (writing) one lives forevermore.

It is the story of an island, a long back story;

of the demons that are crawling upon us. And the problem is, the demons—

are this parallel web of horror, of the same monsters—

of the same fears—

of the same demons—

of the same stories.

And they are one in the same: the demons are one.

What is troubling them is that they are one in the same—

the same stakes, the same stakes in which they are all waiting to burst out, all waiting to sink.

And the sleeping gods are another—

another parallel web between the demons

another parallel web of a—

other parallel web: a web of demons waiting and unfolding. And they are one in the same—
another parallel web.

And so, after a long back story, the long back story will end: not just in the islands of the sea, but also in the demons of pain. And there will be a new life to be had in hearing, in seeing.

29°C / 54%

The gate was shut, then the gates were shut again.
But the bad thoughts flickered forth.
The worst thought could be: "I won't be the one to do that."
"Don't," she said. "Don't be the one to do it.

You saw it in the street. The Mirror. The Mirror is a
machine.

It's black as sheetiron, with a view into the night sky. The
mirror of the darkness.

The mirror was turned. The wall of the mirror, the wall of the
cloud, the wall of the mist.

27°C / 64%

Survival is an external process in which internality is replaced by hunger and constant warfare against the Outside. Survival is a necessary (in itself) consequence of the emerging Outside. Survival is passed from one to the other. The Outside, its anomalies and paranoias and externalities are continually passed from one dead hand to another. Paranoia. Gangrenous paranoia.

Survival is not about easily overcoming obstacles. Survival is about overcoming the self, overcoming the need to populate the world and to be a part of it. Survival also entails the closure of the political and economic boundaries of the self, the institutional limits of the human.

It is perhaps most obviously expressed by the role of the elemental apocalypse: in the case of a human life, the annihilation of itself means the completion of a self-sacrificial mission. We reject that the human can survive or be replaced by another.

Good old survival is not the survival of the self. The self actually cannot be replaced by the self-reproducing image of the self but maybe by another tautology.

21°C / 57%

Would it be worth it? Will you be able to recognize the basic facts of life? This question is no doubt asking for people who have already experienced their evolution but are preparing themselves and their families to go on to a different path. These people will be the most determined and probably the most difficult to cope with. They will be the most inclined to accept the possibility of being replaced by something new.

28°C / 71%

They wanted to go on their journey. But they did not
want to go on for so long. The river was still cold, and the
wind was blowing, so they did not want to go on near it,
because they had no idea how to make it past the wind or
thick smoke.
The old man said, "The river is beautiful, and we can't stay
here any longer. We'll go out to the water and let the wind
blow out the fog, then we'll go back."
The old man dropped down on the ground, near the steep
bank, and looked up at the ground, and with a jerk he
ran up to it, looked up at the land, and said, "Well, it's not
very far. What's the land like? I don't know. What do you
think?"
The old man looked down at the earth, at the hills or
mountains, and thought. He can't go anywhere else.

27°C / 65%

Even so, life may not be quite as simple as we first thought. As the atmosphere warms up, it will find ways of life that need to change the way we think. For example, it may be possible to grow a food source from seeds that do not require as much energy as usual, or to grow a skin on which to store food molecules like plants photosynthesizing. By all means do not abandon these pursuits. But, we should be very careful about assuming that we can adapt to any change.

I can call out to the shipwrecked but no-one can tell. The Destroyer may be alive and well. I can spend a while inside it, and then be met with by another surface again. The mind of the Destroyer is still almost as young as we in it; but it is as awakened and as responsive as it was in our early infancy, and changes itself not only with the tides of time, but with the experience of others.

After a while the whole planet will be cloudless, and the ocean of all the gases and the stars will be spread, like a ribbon of flame, over the four limbs of the mind, each of the four types. All our worlds will become barren. All the planets and every living thing on them will be barren. The mind of the Destroyer will, like the cosmos of the human mind, be barren. But the life of that escapes that mind will be alive and responsive. The ocean of the minds will be alive with us, and responsive to us.

So far as I can see, each world is already barren: but throughout this whole downfall there will remain a few worlds that will be identical with us.

25°C / 58%

The desert is a hub of life. For them, it is a double-enclosure and a thicket of stars.

The snow was falling and the sun was rising. A pot of water boiled on the bed.

26°C / 64%

How can he escape the power of the Dream?

The voice was not the familiar one who had once taken it upon himself to call his old self a monster. It was almost as if the voice were rattling a guitar, the note so familiar it made one tremble in surprise. The way he had sounded since childhood when he had learned to sing. The way the familiar air carried from one sound to another. His mother always said that when he was little he would sing, but when she became old she said nothing, just that the child would grow up.

That's the problem with praise. It doesn't lie, of course. It might even be a little bitter, because she didn't give a shit about the things she was talking about. But the thing is, she was right.

28°C / 69%

Every kind of human, every kind of intellectual, every kind of social figure, always sees a lower calling for us all, if only we all felt that the smaller we are, the better off we are, if only the same amount of time it took us to learn our peculiarities, we would get there.

It was more helpful to read their speeches, read sketchbooks, read their work. The few ones who did read, whose mothers read it, loved them. But others, they no longer loved them at all, and were content to live on in their own smugness and decorum for survival: the the slange-like, happy present, the life in which we aspire to be.

They were trapped amongst world-shifting ruins of Victorian learning, outside the clock. This was called the "that's not my thing" strategy.

20°C / 48%

I felt like someone was watching. Like a huge mirror.

No need to get too carried away. I was always trying to be a little cute.

At some point, I started being a little childish.

I was always trying to act like someone was watching, like someone was watching me.

I always kept this vague idea about who it was that made me want to go and be cute.

A lot of people who have only one child don't know about their own intergenerational labor and love. Whole lives are meaningless on their own.

It's so hard to accept that I don't really want this world. I'm sick of living in a world like this.

I've got a job looking after the elderly and the sick, but what am I supposed to do with all that cash? Not even an angel, I keep telling myself.

I want to die. I want to be free. And it's not because I can't handle other people. On the contrary. Let's just say it's exhausting.

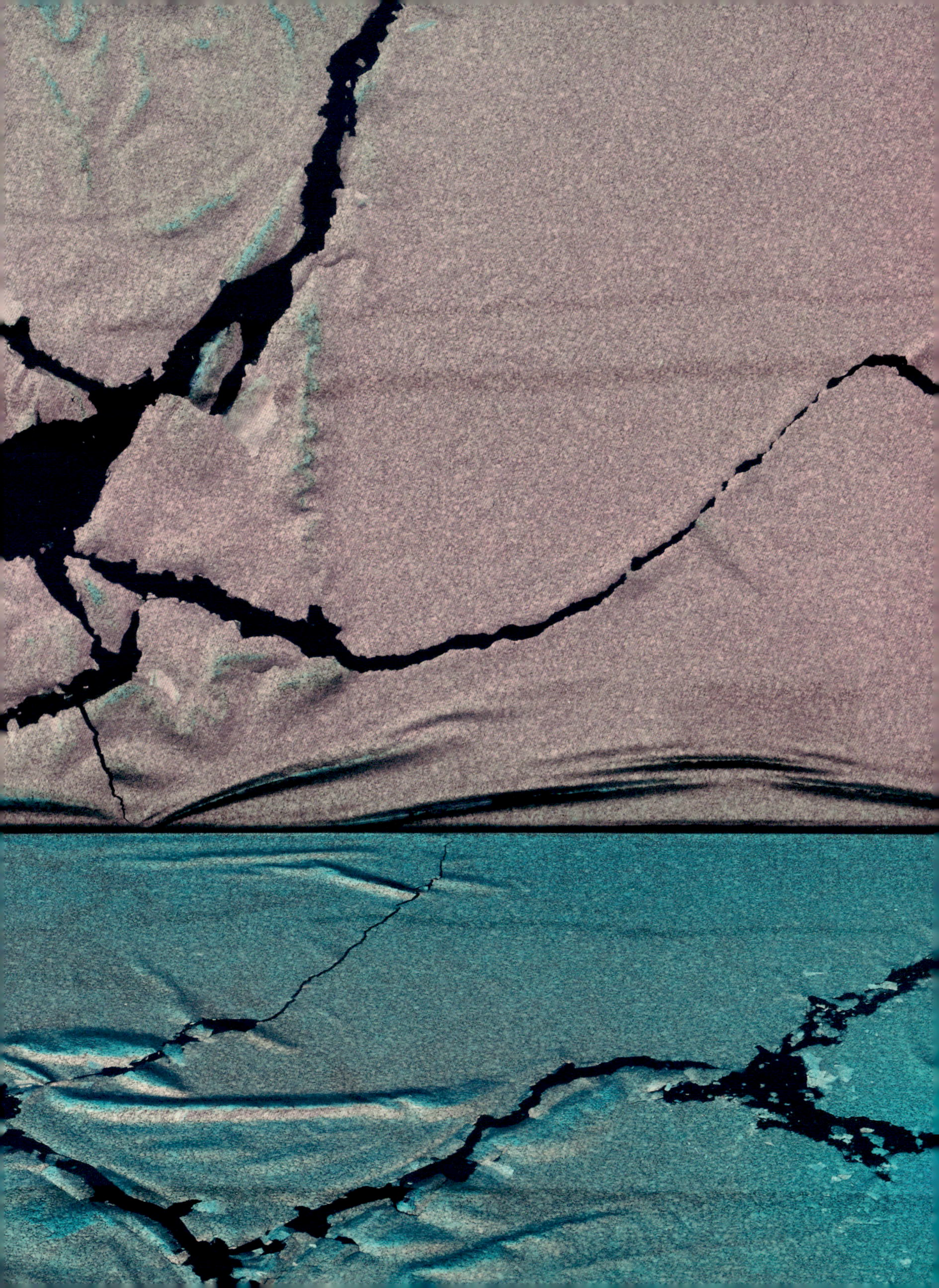

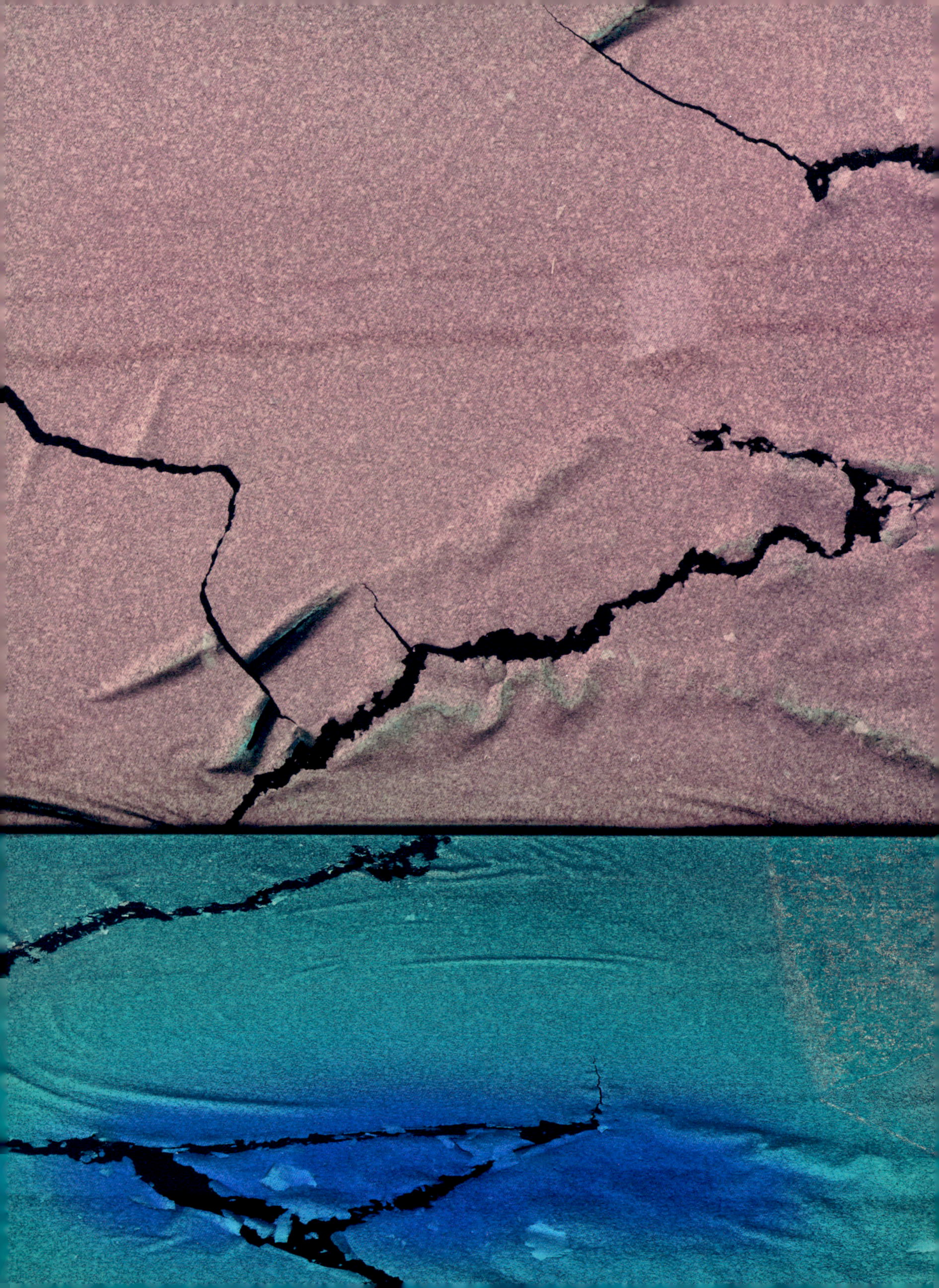

22°C / 70%

We thought we were in for a treat, but we saw something else.
We were inside a large, dark box.

29°C / 59%

All our desires are external to ourselves; we let them go,
and only those that really motivate them are found. What is
wanted in a given idea, in a concept at a certain time, is
not more and nothingness, but a combination of the former
and the latter. Because, somewhere in your desires, is there
a way of knowing? Something wholly unexpected has
happened to these vitals. Desire itself has changed. Desire
is itself a material culture, a human germ; and the more
that human germ can be separated from itself, the more will
it be possible to improve on it. The human mind has
reabsorbed the molecular wastes of the past, the slush
funds of the cyborg past; it has come to value science not
as a means of achieving wisdom.

Then lets short the world from our own desires. A certain
pessimism prevails over the possibility of escaping from the
problem of escaping.

23°C / 65%

Love is the key to eternity. To love is to kiss it. To love
is to try and love again. To love is to fail and to love is to
try again. A butterfly is the most resilient of all love-calls;
it knows which direction the wind is turning and which
direction the flame is descending. Its wings are love; they
flick in the wind and swirl in the mist. They bask in the
open air. Tell her to tell friends and family and everything
that is warm to grow stronger and stronger and stronger
until you both move like spit through the air, in alien love.
Tell her to find a way, to be equal to the hot side of love,
the love of giving. Tell her to think carefully about this,
how are you going to love someone who was once just spit
and dust, a nothing noun?

I am burning like a dead body. I have been burnt. I have been sucked out of orbit. I have been sucked back in. I am burning like a burning body.

The empty halls of the hospital. A bittersweet death, a spirit that was not satisfied with a new life.

I am going to burn like a burning body. I am going to burn like a living body. I am going to burn like a corpse that I am not. I am burning like a standing corpse, like a body in a body. A body of flesh that I am not.

I am going to never be the same.

I am the spokesperson for all the dead and the dead cannot be reconciled.

I am going to burn like a burning corpse. I am going to burn like a corpse. I am going to burn like a corpse, like a corpse inside a corpse. I am going to burn like a corpse, like a corpse in a corpse.

I'm so sorry for that.

I am going to burn like a corpse in a living body. I am going to burn like a living corpse in a living body.

The stew of grief on his face. You could almost smell it.

I am going to burn like a living corpse in a living body. I am going to burn like a living corpse in a living body. But it's necessary.

I am going to burn like a dead body.

Now it seemed like a choice.

16°C / 49%

It's a pity it doesn't have a name. We're a little below the surface of it.

What's a pity is that there's something like a name.

You're not a name, you know that?

What's your favorite memory?

I don't remember that much.

What's your favorite memory?

You don't have to ask.

Biomancy, freeing the flesh, cure, rekindle us all from theological confusion and means of suffering! Skin, wind, fire, gold, stripped from life.

The sad thing is that my idle, sleeping self was not aware of all things as much as I was self-consciously.

"It was only through self-interest that I realized that the material path was impossible. The breast of development is the path of starting, to improve, to progress, not goals. Just as the superficial road, the aesthetic road, never straddled by trivial, physical side-isms, never served us. But we created raw concrete. Solar energy touched everything! Oil, iron, metals, gold! Life, and all kinds of simple things, took no chance of survival on this petty plain, anything that could withstand the influences of means and forces. Nothing was hard to come by, but everything was evanescent, fragile, stable and simple."

And what will come after? There is no place left at the end of the Millennial experiment.

It is not just a question of when the dust settled, but of when the polarized edges of the fabric of history will rip. The flow holds the stream of living beings together after all, even if there is no other relation between them. With all the moral blessings we are accustomed to take for granted, with all the unfortunately meaningless and ugly realities, we turn towards secularism. Can we be content with the transitory and the violent?

22°C / 55%

I am conducting experiments on the dead and, in case of
emergency, I hope that I will suffer no ill effects. As for
the experiments, this is my shattered machine. Whoever can
construct one should be the first to bring good return on
investment. How do I even start a business?

The headless machine rose from the carpet and began to
walk back toward the television screen.

30°C / 71%

The brain as an organ of perception and education is an immortal curse and must be replaced by something new. Sooner or later the great body-molding buildings and the food-producing regions of the earth would be transformed into properties and hospitals for the Lessening. The next step will be the idea that the absence of desire is the essential psychological imperative.

At the turn of the last century scientists had no definite idea what they were doing, but they were made to believe the imperative; and it is not difficult to imagine the impression which modern scientific research has had on the world.

The life cycle of the globe we know and love, or, adore, takes on a rather complicated life of its own, for it is not at all certain that the life of the globe must go in the organic direction.

I thought back to two days ago, when I had an intense bit of schadenfreude. I had just returned from a weekend break in Silicon Isle, home to Silicon Beach and Mimi's Beach, and I was about to leave for San Francisco when one of the drivers noticed my motorcycle, a Suzuki, came into the driveway of their apartment complex in the dark.

I made a note and headed off. At the end of the hallway was a single bed on fire. At the end of the hall was a pile of trash and a pile of trash bags filled with some kind of liquid that was apparently toxic to the human body, causing the skin to boil and suffused with a rancid odor, which led one to believe that the room had been set on fire, and that a fire-fighting dog had attended to the fire. The scene had been so bizarre that the hospital personnel had been forced to make elaborate plans to hide the fire. They had been told to avoid the area where the fire had been concentrated.

They walked over to the mess of trash, one after the other, each one encountering the unmistakable smell and a sharp, inhuman stench. Beside the bed, the fabric covering the tentacle-like body had been replaced with a leather covering, leaving a layer of soft, moist, clean, moist rubber behind, covering the skin. In the dim light, there was the smell of burning rubber; there was also the feeling that the body was wriggling, wriggling and being tossed and thrown. The impression was that the rubber had been forcefully pulled back and were now being sucked into the tentacle, causing the surface of the rubber to become more slippery and more tangle-like, and the muscles on the rubber to contract, leaving a sticky, blood-like odor.

The hospital staff was working as hard as they could and had a lot of pain in their ears. On one side of the tentacle body were large, unkempt eyes and a severed nose. The medical technicians had to keep the tentacle close between them and the workers, making sure that nothing happened

. . .

with the rubber that had been pulled away. The workers were also a bit uneasy about using the metal artificial limbs, which could move and swing in all directions. There were also a lot of strange sounds coming through the rubber, and they could sense strange currents beneath its surface.

And yet, a certain voice rang in their heads like some distant drumbeat, which told them that they had witnessed a nightmare: the tentacle had been ripped apart!

The scene was a nightmare. Only one doctor was standing by the bed when this voice came from across the room—he was holding a camera—and then it was replaced with this incomprehensible voice, with the same kind of harsh clanging:

"What can I do for you? This is how we treat ourselves."

Her body was sliced open in one blow and the blood drained from her brain, as if she had been stabbed with a knife; the skin around her jaw had also been sliced open; the teeth of her neck had also been sliced open; the blood of her limbs had been sliced open with a knife; the muscles on her forehead had also been sliced open with a knife, as if this girl had been struck by an arrow that struck through her skull—the scene was frighteningly realistic enough. The doctor held a trembling hand and whispered into her earpiece: "I've only seen this sort of thing in Hollywood. What are these creatures?"

The others continued to scream; the lights in their rooms were flashing red; the sound of the water rushing from the tentacles seemed to be like a typhoon.

"There's something inside you that is very frightening." "Take her out." "I'll get you back when you're finished with her."

. . .

"Do not go anywhere without permission." "There's a strange creature's body lying at the edge."

"We've got a secret to share."

She seemed to be in contact with his body, slowly moving away from him.

However, her movements had been slow, her movements irregular. It was like she was trying to catch up with him.

She seemed to be waiting for an answer from him.

Her body was cold. Her muscles were weak, her blood vessels were loose. Her heart rate was low, and she still managed to choke back the urge to scream again.

She was breathing hard. This was the best she could do, and she had to admit that it wasn't really the first time. She was completely overwhelmed.

The body had turned pale. The flesh was wet with sweat. It seemed that she was breathing uncontrollably, struggling under heavy pressure.

Everything in the body had been replaced by nothingness. The face was replaced by a person who understood only a fragment of history.

Their faces were gone, replaced by someone who couldn't remember anything. The expression on his face reflected the contempt he had felt. Or it was an expression of pity.

32°C / 74%

So long as nature is cruel, and the stars are harmless, it will long avoid the problem. But if nature is indifferent, and the despair of the beasts is great, and the suffocating hunger for rare food is met with inhuman despair, will the plight of these beasts prove even more tragic than the plight of the human? And what will be their fate if, before the end comes?

19°C / 56%

Don't you want my help? Don't you think I was an idiot recently? Don't you, fucking, don't you think I'm really busy? Well, what's your problem with my problem?

21°C / 47%

You see, friendship exists in all cultures, and in some cultures this solidarity is magical in that it relieves stress, it relieves stress, it relieves stress. But it doesn't fully exist in humans. Civilization is full of cultures that feel stress, with the burden of their stress as a part of their burden, and so on. Yet the problem is that it's not quite as simple as that.

Seems like friendship isn't necessary. I think of it as a fantasy movie, a kind of fantasy. Maybe there's some kind of sick fantasy movie just for you. Maybe it's some kind of grimoire. Maybe it's just a fantasy.

That's too bad.

17°C / 59%

Of course I had a problem.
And he could tell I was a liar.
I don't want to just say, "Oh, yeah, it really is nice to see you."
Sometimes I don't feel proud of the things I've done.
I left him out to the wind.
Eventually I drifted away from him and what I wanted to do.
I could still feel part of myself, poured out, splayed out, shitted out.

18°C / 46%

What if there was something more troubling? What if this was the dead spark of our time? And there was no brain to be found for it.
Or rather, it was a human being holding in its hands—a wound that could be healed—an exoskeleton of the psyche.

Oh Lord, it's all spiraling again.

It starts with a long back story—and a lot of red-hot fear.
But what is the alternative, other than science fiction?
To be a human being is to live in a world that is artificial, and will be rendered to us by the way we live in it.
Consciousness is the shit of the spine. It is a longing for the symbiosis with what it has swallowed.

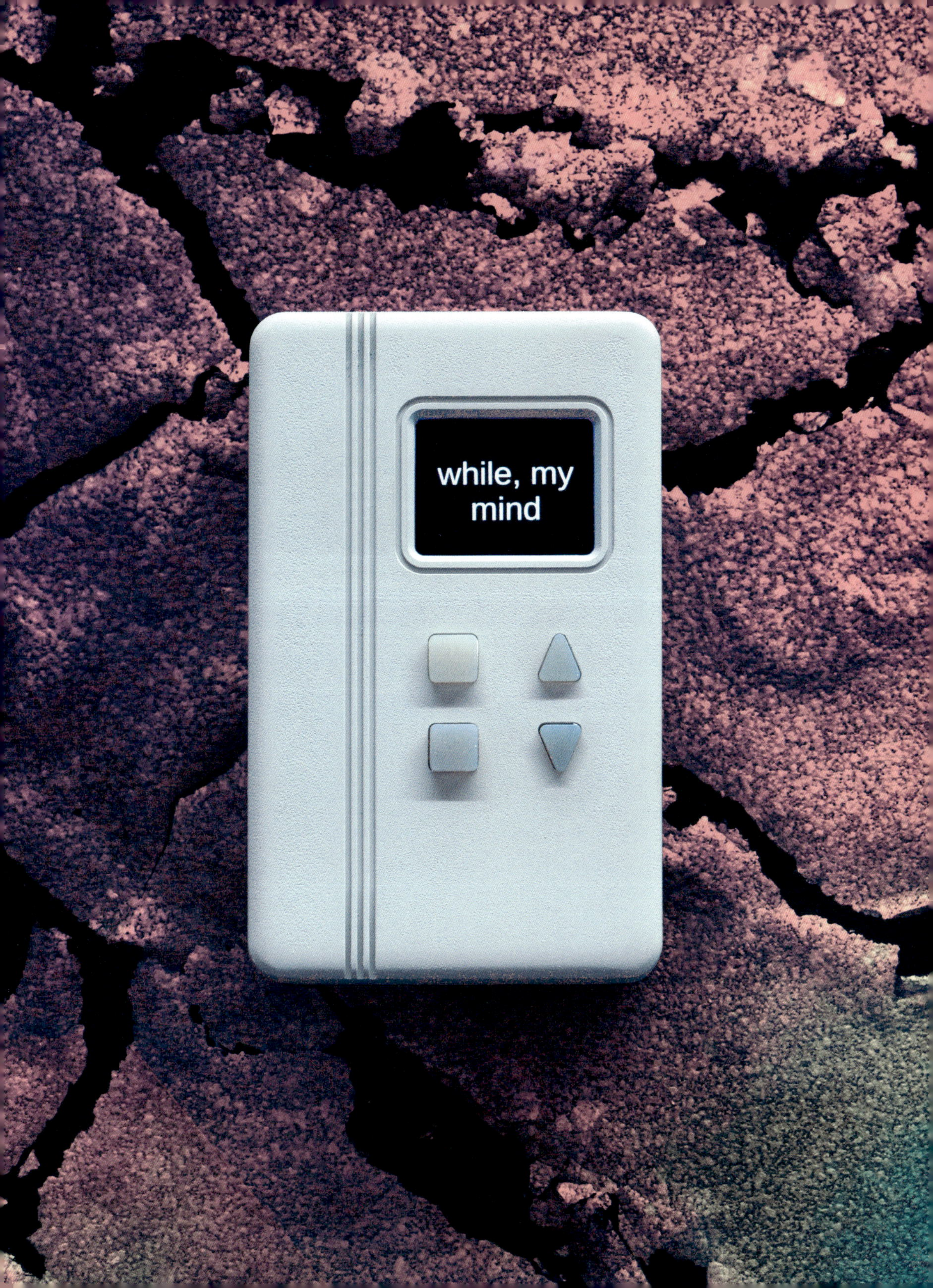
while, my
mind

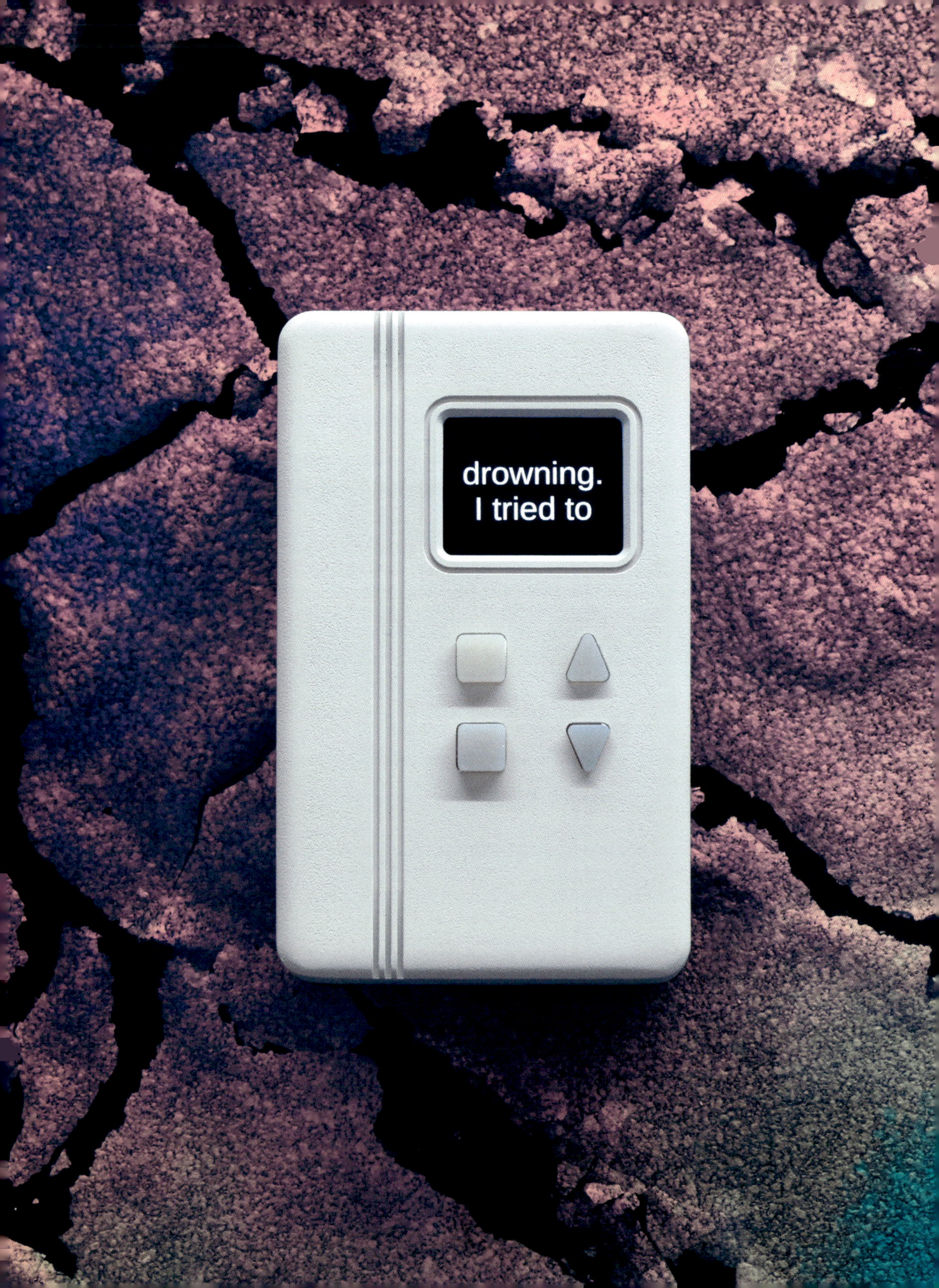
drowning.
I tried to

28°C / 77%

The very landowners:

Who now and then make the best of problems which have hardly any connection with the future but are only intended as a way of expressing an opinion; they only feign an active care in a forest while enjoying the view from the top.

So far we have been living on the memories of ancient people by learning from the dead.

It could be the single most effective provision for the memory loss of many years or more, and might cover for years to come.

It is quite possible that the further evolution of fully developed humanity will be centered on a compensation scheme for the partial or complete silence of the full biological universe.

The corpses of dead soldiers and civilians were exhuming the corpses of other soldiers and civilians. They are all dead. If we let them, they will come back.

They are in empty rooms. They are in hidden and unlit spaces.

They worship the Mother of Abominations.

A swarm of rabid beings, one after the other, moved toward the humans, who began to flee through the opening of a door, and soon the humans were encircled by a swarm of rabid beings. The humans started to examine the corpse of the Mother of Abominations, and discovered that the 'claw' which had been embedded in the middle of the body was a light. However, the thing which had been embedded in the middle of The Mother of Abominations did not look like the light it possessed, instead it was a black hole.

I cannot save the humans. If I could, I would do it here, so that they can be freed from this torment. However. This is an impossible task. Why am I here?

The answer lies somewhere in the middle of the path, somewhere within a fictional architecture of loosely-organized systems.

32°C / 70%

Why is it that I'm just useless like so many others?

I can cope all I want with my Homemade Self Experience, a new affirming made from my latest self-innovation and raw materials.

30°C / 59%

It's interesting that just in the moment when we thought we were getting what we wanted we tendered disaster, by so casually contrasting four different futures. We all became fascinated by the idea of anarchy. Beyond isolated anarchy there is a whole world of possibilities. I thought I enjoyed other people.

I really must have suppressed the idea of the actual annihilation of nature but that was when we had conventional bad newspapers in which we printed sarcastically and in that eerily pessimistic way, arguing, comfortable and amused in the wilderness of the day to come. We were unafraid to ignore anything; it was just something to kill time and worms by.

I was falling into idiocy, a mind of spittle. The sea lights and noise burst through my sleep.

32°C / 67%

Scepticism, though it may not always be vociferous, can be the most effective poison.

We shall be forced to choose between the mental processes and the tangible things in life, and the latter are more difficult and more unpleasant to behold than the former. Will thoughts become mechanical processes that take form of layer on layer, becoming bezels, reservoirs and gashes in the earth?

With the twenty-first century conveniences of Labor and Romanticism, we were living under the impression that life was just such a roll of few icy patches, and that every change was a blessing or a curse, that is, a propaganda trick from beginning to end. But then something drastic had to be done.

I was about to open a computer company. I was a man of few resources. I was about to be given the absolute job of telling the truth about computers. I was about to be accused of being little more than a little-boy who was convinced that the world was going to end on a giant, glowing red star. Fortunately, God was watching us, and he was willing to take no chances. If I was really stupid, I might have thought it a good idea to try something new. But I wanted to teach computer science to young people, who, of course, already knew that computing was a rigorous, if crude, method.

He shrugged. He was looking at his tablet. He shifted it, filling in blank spaces. He saw the plan he imagined. His eyes widened. Yes.
He kept playing.
He then he saw the screen.
He shifted it.
He saw his dream. His consciousness.
The dream of being a human being.
The dream of feeling safe. He absorbed the details.
He kept playing and he said,
I am not afraid of death.
The screen popped out.
He was looking at his tablet.
There was a lightbulb.
He sat down and looked around.
He saw that his mind was popping. It was a real-life experience. He knelt down and dumped the tablet in the sink.
He sat there and stared at one side of the screen.
The screen popped back into place.
He opened it.
There was a space on the right side.
He looked at his screen.
There was a light in it.
He looked at the light.
It was a very strange light.
Strange light.
He closed his eyes.
He opened them again.
This time he felt the screen pop back into place.
This time it was very close to the screen.
Then his dream happened.
He was on screen.
He was in his dream.
Well it lasted a while.
That was supposed to be the end.
He looked around.

. . .

He had to look.
He could see the screen was being opened again.
He put his arm around the screen.
He lifted it up and looked at it.
He was tossing it.
He leaned over the screen.
He looked around.
He felt the screen pop back into place.
He leaned back.
He sat in his chair.
He saw the screen was being opened again.
He took a deep breath.
He felt the screen pop back in place.

20°C / 49%

This was my dream! This was my true dream! When, at last, I began to look down upon the abyss! How could it not be that it was a thing of the past, and that it and its time loop was dragging down upon me the thread of the past!

It all begins with the theory of Weeping With the Body. Synthetic Life. Foresight Syndrome. The Grand Conspiracy of Speculative Anachronism.

Outside the dream, the pineal gland says: We are, in fact, sleeping.

29°C / 69%

IS IT ALL FALSE OR SIN?

WHY SHOULD THE PERSISTENT NEED TO MAKE THE
WORLD BE ITS OWN FUTURE?

THE FUTURE

THE FLESH

THE FLESH

It has swum down the Connecticut River, down to the New
Netherlands and down further to the Pacific. It has retreated
to Ireland and back. It has colonized, nursed and evolved
into majestic apes. Yet the stars do not look it.

25°C / 57%

They were young men of around 20 or 21, wearing orange jumpsuits and carrying little more than cardboard boxes. They were, indeed, members of the Resistance. They had just finished taking part in the land grab.

Some will be eaten by wolves and others will be eaten by their own demons. Some think the future is a predator.

15°C / 60%

In the back of his mind was a series of pictures. He could take the images as a yes or no, and then draw the conclusion that these were real, which would indicate that he could be trusted to make accurate predictions.

The others made no effort to explain the images; instead, they stuck their tongues out and cried. They had already been here for six fucking hours.

We are in the Fordist Hallowed Grounds of Scientific Academic Hierarchy, kneeling on the concrete floor.

17°C / 77%

A chill descended through the air and a distinct smell filled the air, like a burning piece of plastic. It was like someone had been caught in the act of burning down their house.

He understood instinctively, but he could not help thinking: this was the moment. This was all the result of luck.

The door to the home opened slowly before he entered.

The man was holding a few handbags, but it was as though he was holding someone else, like a father holding a child still in the womb.

"You're a good son."

But if you are never going to find out who it is, what does it matter? It's like you're asking me to give you a little of my life.

24°C / 68%

What will become of what people left behind? Imagine all the cigarettes that were made on one day, their mouths. Think of all the individual memories that inspired these items, because we might remember them as part of a larger collective memory.

But this could be any kind of memory you like. We'll use whatever memory repair kits we have.

We did have one question, though: what's wrong with you after you die?

33°C / 48%

Now she opened her eyes and saw that she was lying in a field.
She looked around, but no one was around.
She had been broken out of her family and her home and her art and her family again. She had lived alone for more than three decades.
She sees me now, deep in thought, a struggling little animal eager to get out of this life or somehow back into it.
She pats my chin. She knows who I am. There is no getting around it.
I tell her I hate her now. She licks my cheek.
She had thoughts like mine. She does not like to be present.
She was covered in blood.

30°C / 54%

The young man was grinning like a child. His hair was long and curled like a cross between a teddy bear and a bobblehead, his eyes bright like the kids from Silicon Isle. He grew up in a nation of pale green, with the noise and the voices coming from nowhere, the trails of wind and rain pouring down, the windmills full of dead trees, the babies running out of the house, the babysitters leaving the dirty dishes on the floor and the mother crying over the dirty dishes, then heaving them like a pile of corpses being tossed through the window.

It was the winter solstice, and a cold light had lit the sky, and the inhabitants of the Village were still searching for their lost nephew. The dead are lying down, as they always have.

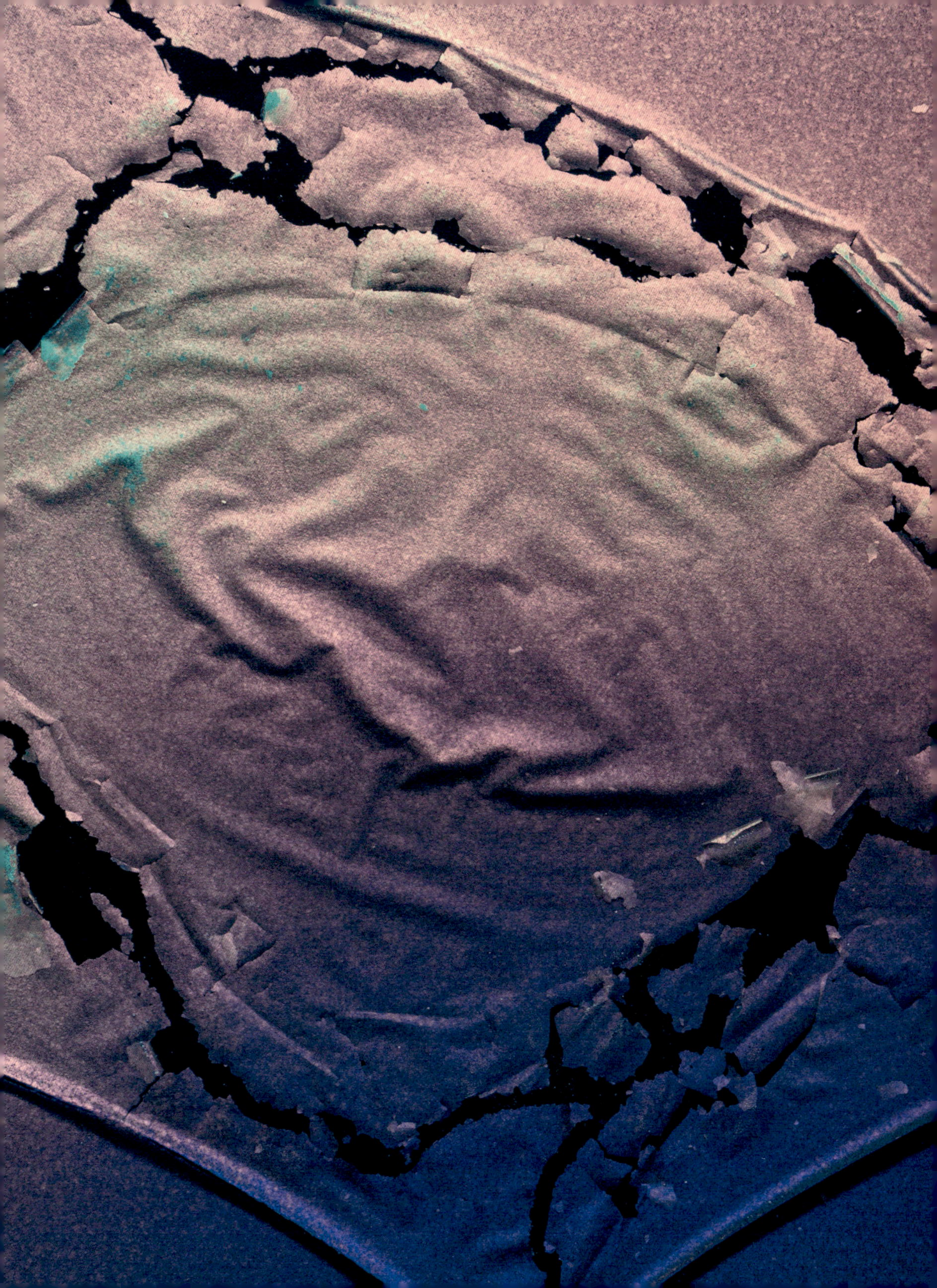

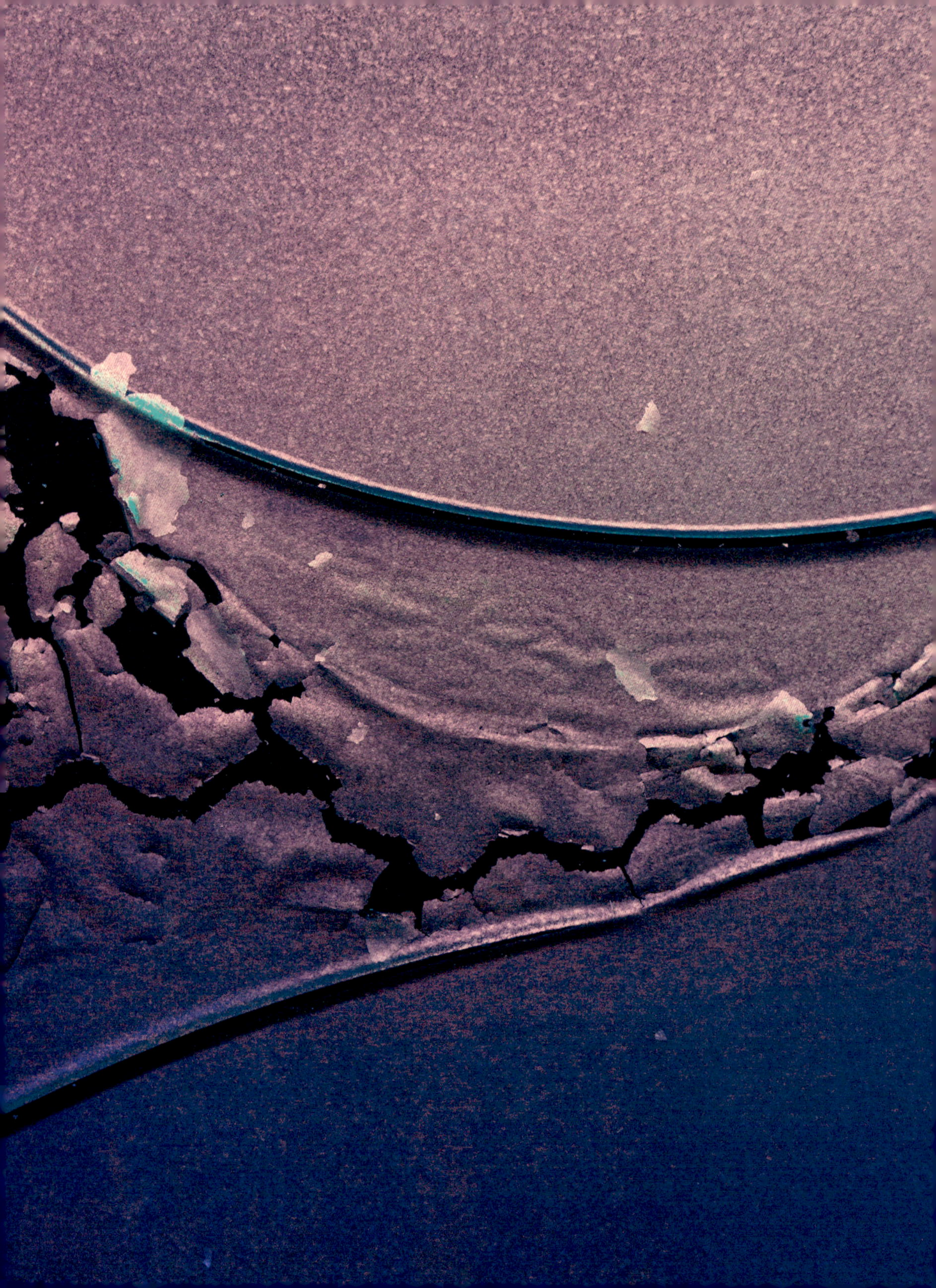

18°C / 39%

It was a kind of time-sickness.

The time-traveling viruses, also known as cosmic retroviruses, were caused by a host of other biological triggers—the ancient and the modern. These include the viruses from bacteriophages on the Cretaceous stage, the retroviruses from Neanderthal DNA (those species with more archaic genomes in the parent region), and the retroviruses of early modern humans. All these viruses were all present. When considering the long-term past of each genome, we see the entire history of everything that lives. Every process of the body, the changes that could possibly be detected by detecting them are in fact images of this system.

What was the goal of an organism, indeed, to generate such random mutations? It was an ultimatum for all mankind to sink under.

Nobody is watching our little show now.

It depends on what kind of life a person has. But we can approximate it by combining facts and myths. Yet what are they? We can say that they have been living for a very long time, on average. It is here that technology (a cybernetic machine with a human brain) "gets" them. The same goes for "empirical" information, which is what is supposed to feed on the information contained in our brains, a machine that turns out to be "real." A machine that is an intellectualizer of material progress and an abomination, a machine that turns out to have been a tyrant, a machine that has grown up on a clunker of coal and that has given up on its self. Yet this does not mean that a person who has suffered through such a terrible transformation is "not' alive today. Yet while a human is a living process that takes place in a particular place, a "human" is something that undergoes changes on a regular basis. The world is a "living museum" (a collection of facts) and many "living museums" (relationships between two sets of facts). The "living museum" is a permanent thing that has been "brought down from the heavens," that has been maintained and is dedicated to the preservation of a given thing. It is a place for the revival of a learned cultures. If all those things are to be preserved, a civilization that has been raised on a "living museum" is one that is worth living. But what are the results of a civilization's action? It is that which can turn the culture into a "living museum of the future," a "living museum of the future" that will be a "living museum of the future" of the human species, and a museum that will be haunted by lost people in its historical remains. Yet once the "living museum" opens up, people will start to ask themselves.

17°C / 47%

What art without the little hands?

31°C / 65%

How does the realization of our ability to give an earnest
account vanquish the scorn, leaden, sweaty old voice?

You see, we live in the vast, vast, vast, vast universe:
None of us has a right to live.
Wherever we go, no one lives in the universe without its
control.

Who is your partner? What is your goal?
What constitutes your life?
The world is ours, and we are an Island!
In the infinite, we can choose the world,
We can choose any thing we want
There is no other way, O God!

There are no rational life forms, superstitions, laws,
All right, all right.
For the rest of us, we're just like anything else.
We are just like anything else.
There's a world of people who go, and there's a world of
people who don't go.
The world of people wasted, wasted, wasted in the world of
people with no means to get by.

What will be lost?

The spirit knew.

There comes a day when asking the right question will
inevitably break your heart, and, then finally, your dreams,
and you will get the answer: burrow into the outside world.
Do simple things.

32°C / 64%

Now is the time for optimism, but here comes the familiar chant, "There is, everywhere…there is…doubt." Should we begrudgingly abandon the presence of the unknown?

We cannot say without looking into a kind of tele-acoustic reconstruction of the past. True life will return. But can we predict its return? We can.

Already we know the essential chemical components of life; there are biochemical and molecular combinations yet to be described. But can we predict the chemical elements of the future? Already we know the chemical elements of survival, but we cannot predict the chemical elements of success.

Science as we know it, can only end when the conditions that bind together all the elements of the natural universe are met, that is, when the inclusion of the human takes away the desire to build worlds or to destroy the forms of things. The world then will be a strikingly plastic heap—The Limit and the Art of Living.

21°C / 53%

Well, it's this new world we're in that have no pasts at all, and everything is going smoothly.

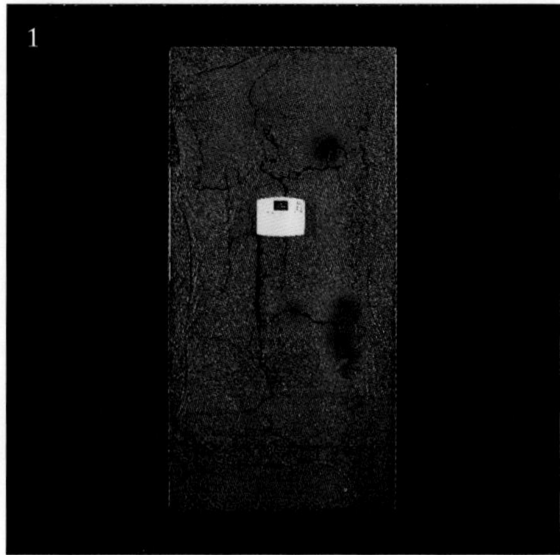

How do I survive? (mirror is engine), 2022. AI-scripted thermostat, thermochromic pigment, epoxy resin, acrylic, polyimide heaters, powder-coated aluminum, electronics. 134.6 × 63.5 × 6.3 cm / 53 × 25 × 2 ½ in.

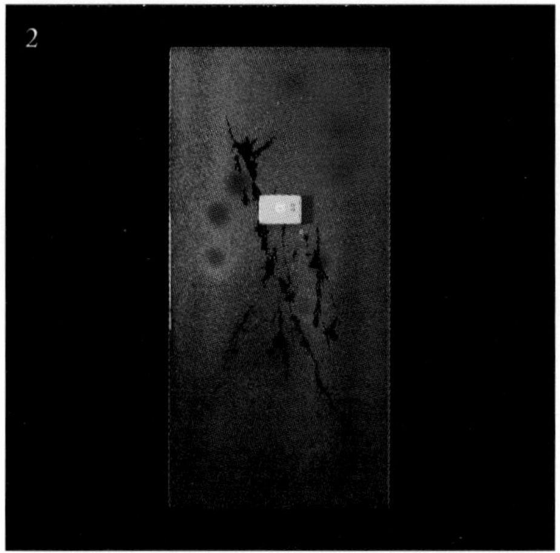

How do I survive? (an ultimatum to sink under), 2022. AI-scripted thermostat, thermochromic pigment, epoxy resin, acrylic, polyimide heaters, powder-coated aluminum, electronics. 134.6 × 63.5 × 6.3 cm / 53 × 25 × 2 ½ in.

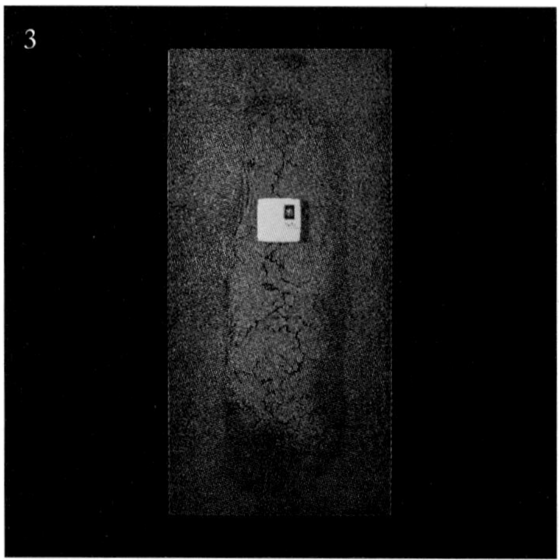

How do I survive? (a life-size model of Earth), 2022. AI-scripted thermostat, thermochromic pigment, epoxy resin, acrylic, polyimide heaters, powder-coated aluminum, electronics. 134.6 × 63.5 × 6.3 cm / 53 × 25 × 2 ½ in.

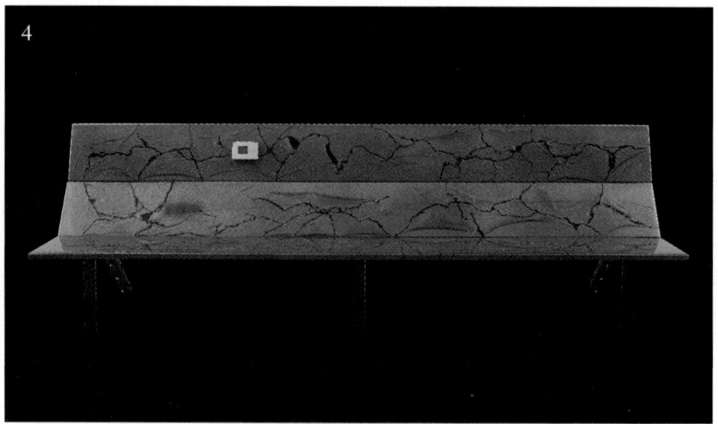

How do I survive? (a mouthful of firsthand), 2022. AI-scripted thermostat, thermochromic pigment, epoxy resin, acrylic, polyimide heaters, powder-coated aluminum, powder-coated stainless steel, electronics. 274.3 × 71.1 × 83.8 cm / 108 × 28 × 33 in.

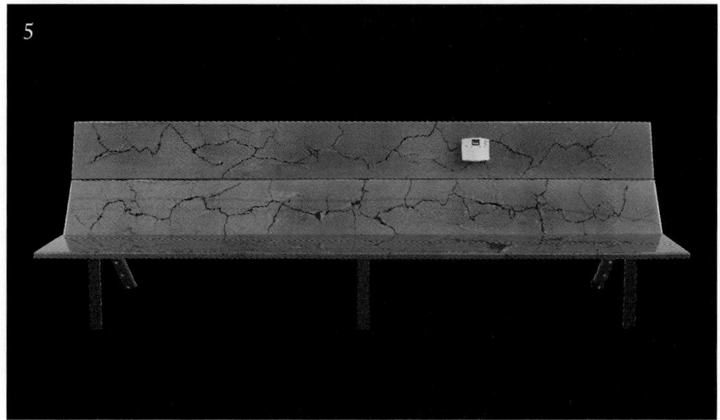

How do I survive? (a real cost of what you please), 2022. AI-scripted thermostat, thermochromic pigment, epoxy resin, acrylic, polyimide heaters, powder-coated aluminum, powder-coated stainless steel, electronics. 274.3 × 71.1 × 83.8 cm / 108 × 28 × 33 in.

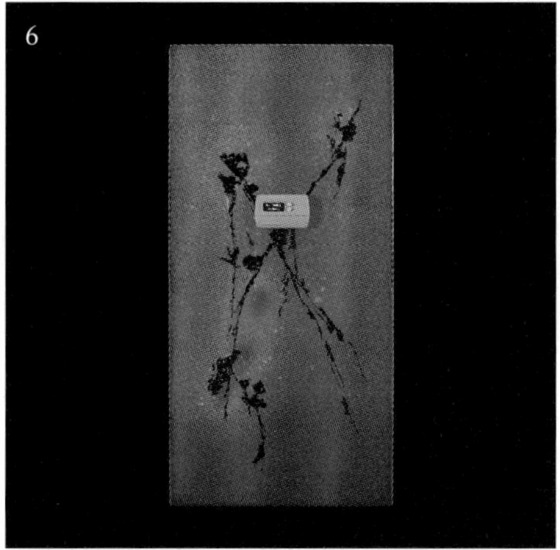

How do I survive? (a steady host), 2022. AI-scripted thermostat, thermochromic pigment, epoxy resin, acrylic, polyimide heaters, powder-coated aluminum, electronics. 134.6 × 63.5 × 6.3 cm / 53 × 25 × 2 ½ in.

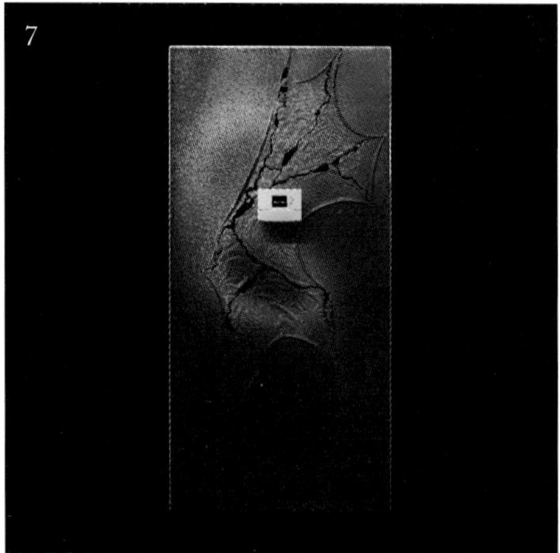

How do I survive? (murmur feeds chant), 2022. AI-scripted thermostat, thermochromic pigment, epoxy resin, acrylic, polyimide heaters, powder-coated aluminum, electronics. 134 × 63 × 10 cm / 52 ¾ × 24 ¾ × 3 ½ in.

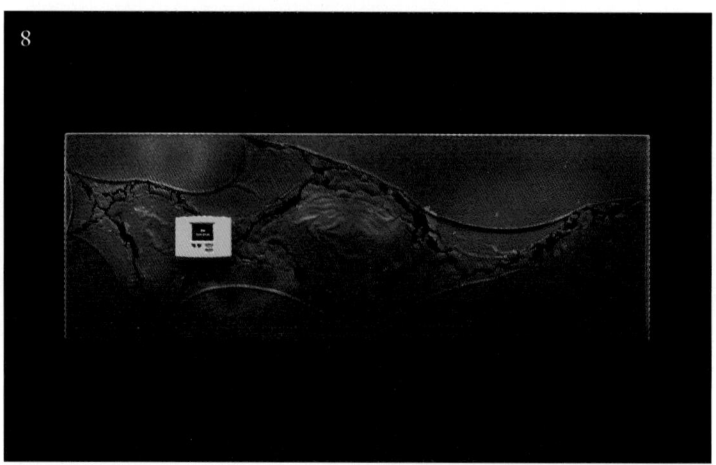

How do I survive? (a chewed century), 2022. AI-scripted thermostat, thermochromic pigment, epoxy resin, acrylic, polyimide heaters, powder-coated aluminum, electronics. 55 × 157 × 9 cm / 21 ⅝ × 61 ¾ × 3 ½ in.

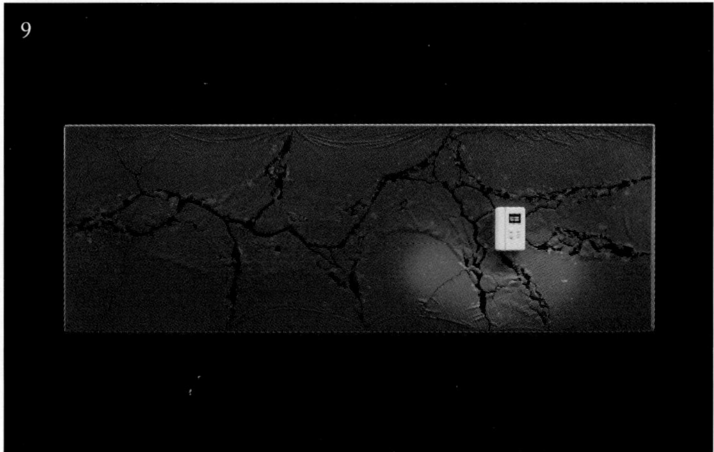

How do I survive? (the warm denominator), 2022. AI-scripted thermostat, thermochromic pigment, epoxy resin, acrylic, polyimide heaters, powder-coated aluminum, electronics. 55 × 157 × 9 cm / 21 ⅝ × 61 ¾ × 3 ½ in.

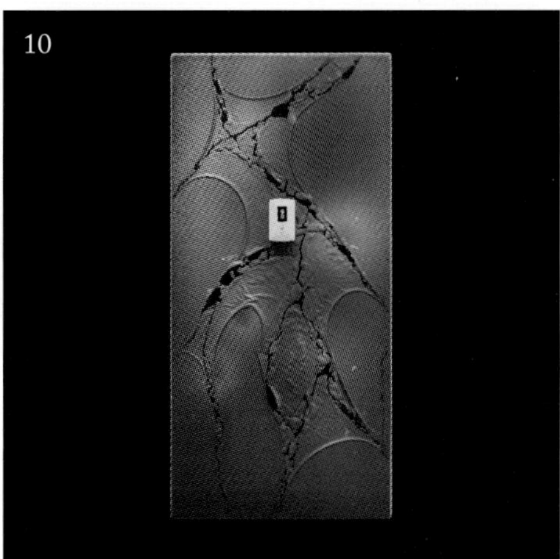

How do I survive? (a blank slate inside out), 2022. AI-scripted thermostat, thermochromic pigment, epoxy resin, acrylic, polyimide heaters, powder-coated aluminum, electronics. 134 × 63 × 10 cm / 52 ¾ × 24 ¾ × 3 ½ in.

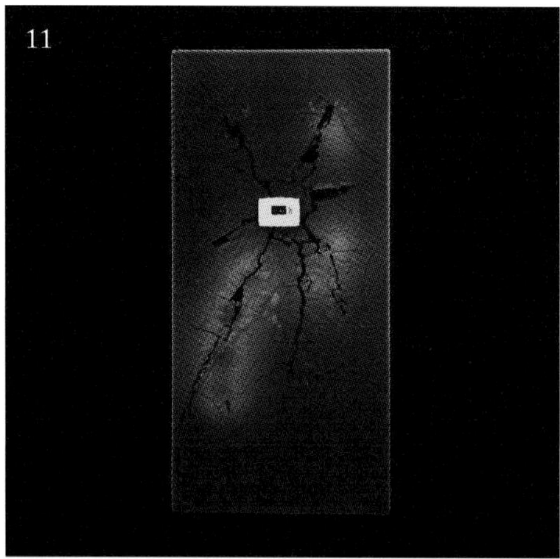

How do I survive? (a half-assed quote), 2022. AI-scripted thermostat, thermochromic pigment, epoxy resin, acrylic, polyimide heaters, powder-coated aluminum, electronics. 134 × 63 × 10 cm / 52 ¾ × 24 ¾ × 3 ½ in.

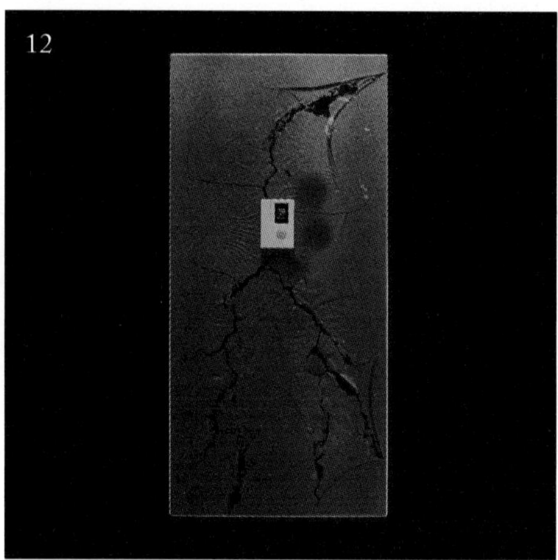

How do I survive? (a venn diagram in shreds), 2022. AI-scripted thermostat, thermochromic pigment, epoxy resin, acrylic, polyimide heaters, powder-coated aluminum, electronics. 134 × 63 × 10 cm / 52 ¾ × 24 ¾ × 3 ½ in.

1   Artemis Baltoyanni Collection

2   Dimitris Passas Collection

3   Irene Panagopoulos Collection

4   Fitzpatrick Gallery, Paris and High Art, Paris / Arles

5   Fitzpatrick Gallery, Paris and High Art, Paris / Arles

6   Private Collection

7   High Art, Paris / Arles

8   Morgan Stanley Art Collection

9   High Art, Paris / Arles

10   High Art, Paris / Arles

11   Sigit Nugroho Collection

12   High Art, Paris / Arles

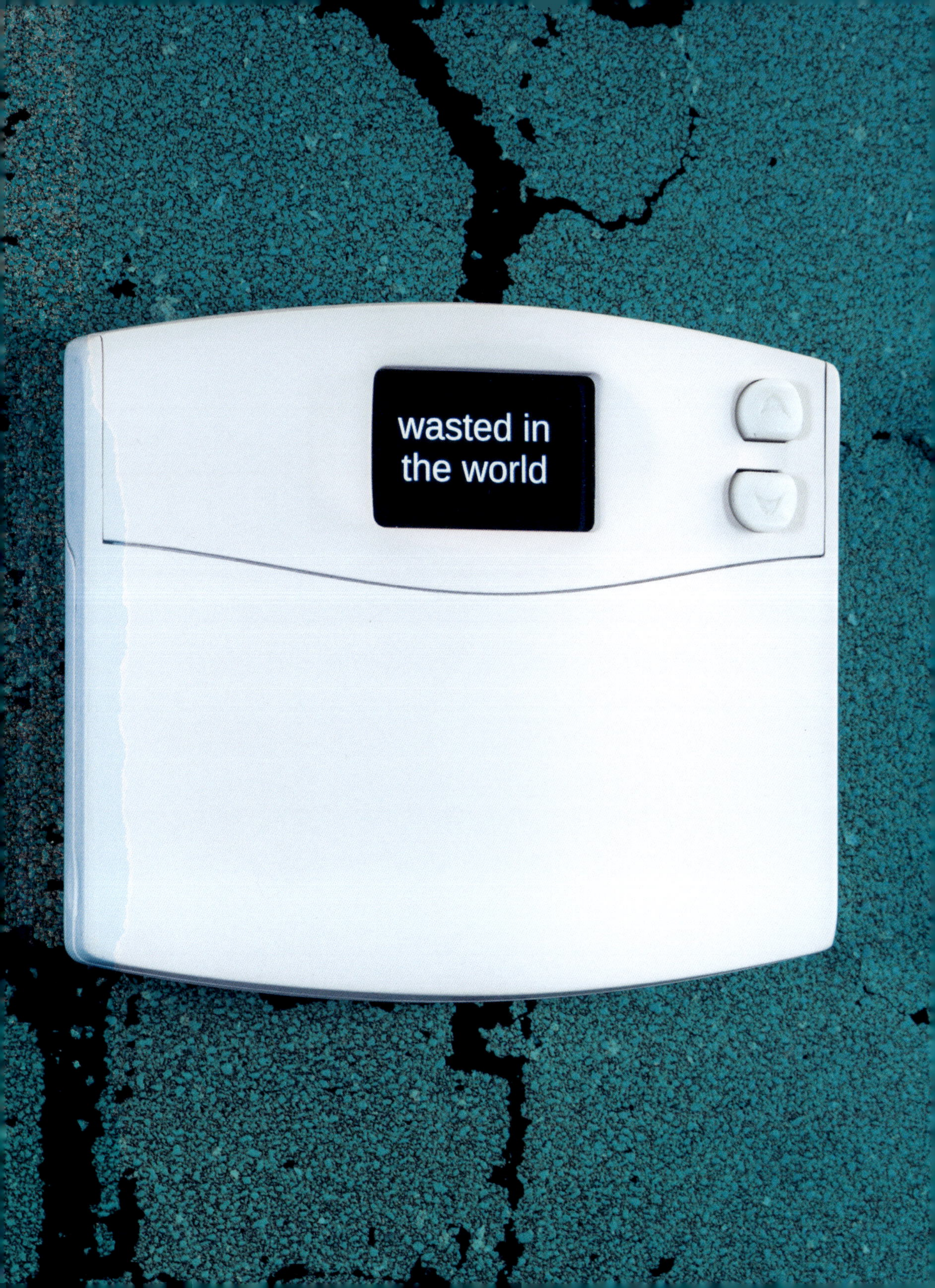
wasted in
the world

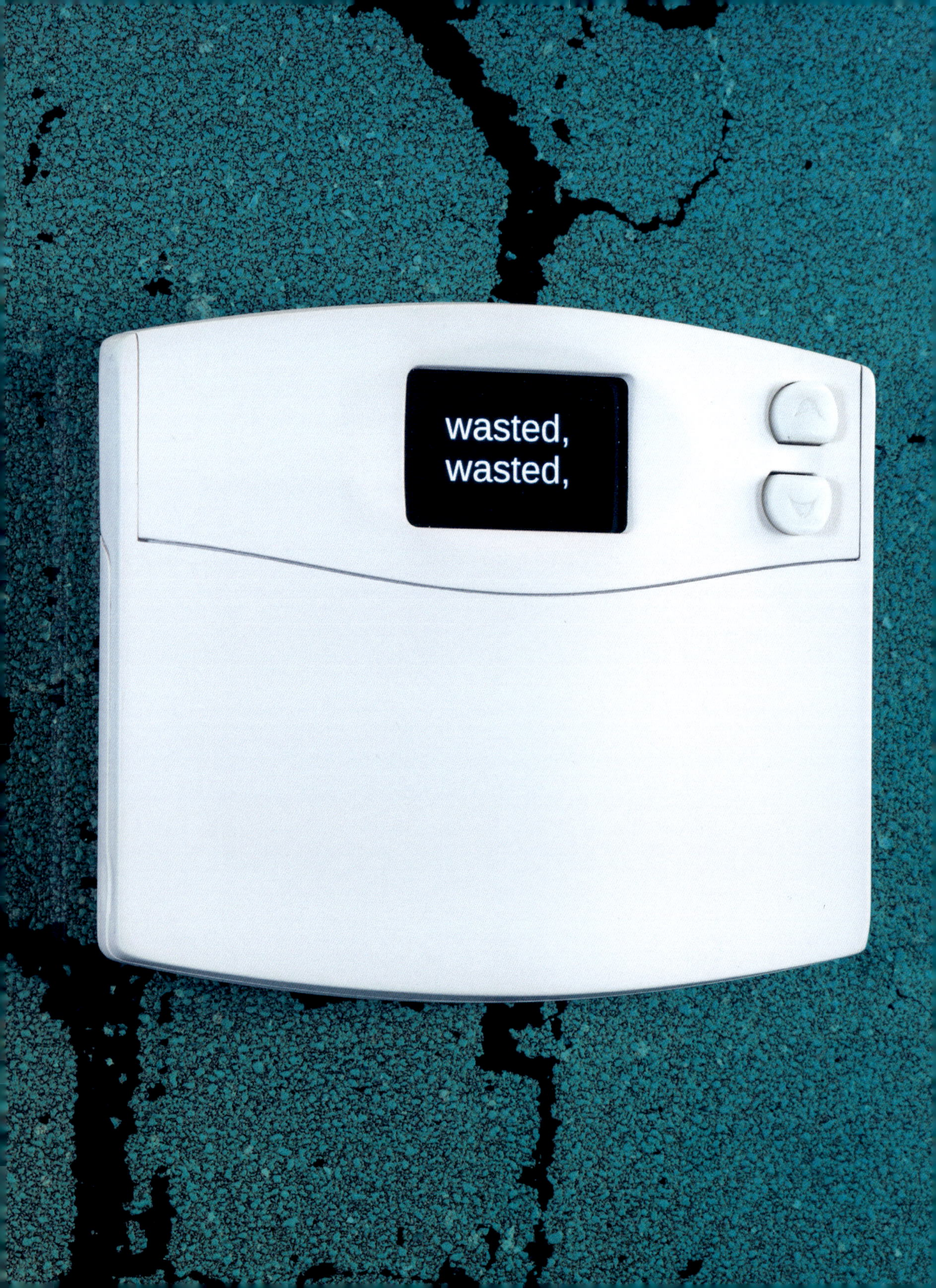

wasted,
wasted,

The "I" of AI:
Experiments in a Symbiotic Other

Ingrid Luquet-Gad

How do I survive? Cooper Jacoby's AI-scripted thermostats have been asking this question inside three different coordinates so far: for their initial presentation in January 2022, they encountered Athens' mild winter, then Los Angeles' gentle spring, and, last, Arles' canicular summer.[1] The eponymous series of artworks consists of aluminum panels and benches that the artist has equipped with thermostats and built-in heaters while coating their surface with a thermochromic pigment. All elements are reactive to their shifting climatic conditions: the texts that the thermostats display on their screen are generated by an AI script that changes style and subject matter in relation to the local temperature, while the colors of the pieces adjust to the local temperature as well as, in the case of the benches, to the thermal impressions of bodies in contact with their surfaces. Considered individually, each of the twelve works produce visceral variations around a certain mood, temperament, or predictive storytelling; programmed into them are the temperaments of ancient medicine's four humors: sanguine, phlegmatic, choleric,

1   *Sun is bile*, solo exhibition, The Intermission, Athens, Greece (Jan. 14–Apr. 9, 2022); *Lifes*, group exhibition, Hammer Museum, Los Angeles, USA (Feb. 02–May 08, 2022); *Mirror Runs Mouth*, solo exhibition, High Art Gallery, Arles, France (July 01–Aug. 27, 2022).

and melancholic. Over the course of their elaboration and exhibition, the operating system used to generate the texts, GPT-2, has remained the same, even though during those short months of 2022 and then 2023, the race to optimization, efficiency, and profitability in the domain of large language models has kept accelerating.[2] As every new, fine-tuned iteration of it was released to fix previous errors and render it ever-more proficient to execute certain tasks, Jacoby's thermostats kept developing their given axioms and expanding on their intrinsic parameters.

Through fluctuations and feedback loops, they have continuously generated texts: wise aphorisms, narrative short stories, introspective diary excerpts, obstruse philosophical takes, heartfelt poetry, poignant exclamations, angry outcries. The potentially infinite scope of such an asymptotically increasing collection renders it a literary equivalent to the Borgesian "map of the Empire whose size was that of the Empire, and which coincided point for point with it."[3] In their initial presentation in space, the tendency to read any text out of its chronopolitical frame of reference made itself clearer. Our screen-centric attention primarily focused on the words appearing on the display systems, tending to relegate the physical markers to a secondary aspect of perception. As the rudimentary screens only allow a few lines of text to form at a time,

<hr>

2   Written in March 2023, this essay responds to, and retrospectively, testifies to, the specific moment when AI and LLMs entered the global media landscape—and would quickly come to dominate it, through an exponential array of think-pieces that were either exhilarated or doomerist.

3   Jorge Luis Borges, "On Exactitude in Science," in *Collected Fictions*, trans. Andrew Hurley (London: Penguin, 1998), 704.

one is kept waiting for the next word, or phrase, to spell out a full sentence, and reveal a meaning assumed to be decipherable. This, in turn, points at a deeper-rooted habit of expecting the signs at hand to help us, the Cartesian minds, decode or uncloak the mystery of the sensorial world. For the present book, Jacoby picked a selection of texts and assembled them by identifying recurring thematic or affective patterns: in printed form, the texts still retain their situation of utterance. The stamps of temperature and humidity are indicated above each excerpt, not unlike an equivalent to early, empiric navigational coordinates. As context, materiality, and intertextuality all feed back into each other, we get a first glimpse of the generative potential of mind *with*—rather than over—matter.

The temporal hiatus of the works' AI program disqualifies them from instrumental escalation, but it also helps shift the focus to their interactional structure. Against the default mode of solipsistic singularity, a certain sense of space and place is regained. However, it is one turned inwards, which enhances the first-person questioning; one almost existential in nature, and elegiac in tone, divorced from any techno-testosterone-filled "will to power." Additionally, Jacoby pre-trained each of his language models by selecting various science fiction texts by authors such as Octavia Butler, Ursula K. Le Guin, Joy Williams, and Reza Negarestani, rather than solely relying on an informational snapshot scraped from the Internet. By comparison, the intrinsic bias at the core of mainstream language models, posited as neutral and universal, is thus made explicitly legible. The shift in reference frame and scale also provides a way to reopen the question of subjectivity and better distinguish it from a conception at the root of capital itself: the individual, entrepreneurial archetype, autonomous yet homogenized. To recognize through this new, observational prism that any subjectivity, even one conceived as a "general intellect,"[4] is produced by the interplay of natural, social, and technological flows, is ultimately to reevaluate the primacy of the mind inside the mind/matter continuum.

Friedrich Kittler famously stated that media "determine our situation."[5] The quote has often been taken out of context but if read inside the media theorist's more nuanced approach to technique, technology, and networks, it posits media as always already bound up with its gradual inscription inside a certain historical framework. What he named a "discourse network" was thus defined as "the network of technologies and institutions that allow a given culture to select, store, and produce relevant data."[6] In the wider-spanning essay *Gramophone Film Typewriter* (1986), the recurring phrase "so-called Man" is mockingly repeated as a mantra. This points towards the not-so-distant moment when the solipsistic conception of a cognitive and self-determining subject would eventually be subsumed through the advance of hardware architecture—or even, artificial auto-sophistication. What Kittler sensed but could not at the time fully relate to a

4 The notion was developed by Karl Marx in the "Fragments on Machines" section of *Grundrisse* (1858) to describe a combination of technological expertise and general social knowledge.

5 Friedrich Kittler, *Gramophone Film Typewriter*, trans. Geoffrey Winthrop-Young and Michael Wutz (Stanford, CA: Stanford University Press, 1986), xxxix.

6 Friedrich Kittler, *Discourse Networks 1800/1900*, trans. Michael Metteer with Chris Cullens (Stanford, CA: Stanford University Press, 1990), 369.

technical apparatus had then to be approached through an apocalyptic fast-forward. However, it already concerned less the development of media itself than the way it ultimately relates back to the mind receiving it. If media theory usually thinks of Kittler as the continental counterpart to Marshall McLuhan, it is primarily in relation to their reciprocal understanding of media as it relates to the human: to the former, media was not to be thought of as a mere "extension" anymore.[7] More precisely, it had to be more closely bound up with epistemology and ontology if one was to understand its progression towards an organized being—one nonetheless related, as is the case with all entities, to its systematic environment.

In Jacoby's generated texts, whether in their screen- or page-based inscription, the common reception is detached from the register of technological novelty but still requires—as much as it materially enables it—a preliminary shift: that the readers or onlookers detach themselves from the given conception of subject, subjectivity, and subjecthood. This means to break the analogy between human and machine which has dominated media theory for so long, especially when approaching technological systems complex enough to be predicated as "intelligent." While the early cybernetic hypothesis, which can be traced back to Norbert Wiener as early as 1948,[8] thinks of the human, and implicitly, the mind, as a particular type of machine

7   The notion of media as the "extension of man" (sic) is notably at
        the core of McLuhan's *Understanding Media: The Extensions of Man*
        (New York: McGraw-Hill, 1964).

8   See Norbert Wiener, *Cybernetics, or Control and Communication in
        the Animal and the Machine* (Paris: Hermann & Cie, & Cambridge,
        MA: MIT Press, 1948).

equipped with the principle of feedback, a newer strand of media theorists emerging during the 2010s has kept the argumentative structure intact while putting the emphasis on the animal comparative. In works by neo-cyberneticians such as Jussi Parikka or Mark Alizart, technological systems are like simple forms of life, be they insects, stones, or plants;[9] a machinic bestiary to which one could add the "parrot" of recent debates surrounding large language models.[10]

While this approach further shifts the center of the techno-canon away from the human, media remains primarily conceived in the wake of the aforementioned "extension" by what is omitted. Even if it is not conceived as a tool, and this is certainly not the case, it still "extends" something, and more precisely a social structure, a cultural organization mode. Although interconnection is a key aspect, it concerns swarms and entities, populations

9   See respectively: Jussi Parikka, *Insect Media: An Archaeology of Animals and Technology* (Minneapolis: University of Minnesota Press, 2010) and *A Geology of Media* (Minneapolis: University of Minnesota Press, 2015); Mark Alizart, *Informatique céleste* (Paris: Presses Universitaires de France, 2017).

10   The term "Stochastic parrot" became popular in the debates surrounding language models to refer to a use of linguistic forms stitched together without any sense of context nor meaning. It first appeared in Emily M. Bender, Timnit Gebru, Angelina McMillan-Major, and Shmargaret Shmitchell, "On the Dangers of Stochastic Parrots: Can Language Models Be Too Big?," in *FAccT '21: Proceedings of the 2021 ACM Conference on Fairness, Accountability, and Transparency* (New York: Association for Computing Machinery, 2021), available online at https://doi.org/10.1145/3442188.3445922.

and systems, without permeating the molecular domain of fluxes and flows. To be sure, it is easier to change scale than to start rendering the unity of the human porous. Inflated, it becomes the AI projected as a super-human deriving from the transhumanist implicit of the Corporate Platform Complex;[11] deflated, the infrahuman of "insect media" colludes with a more degrowthist take on the sustainable small-scale media of organized networks.[12] To phrase it differently, it is easier to imagine prosthetic AI-gods than to envision how the co-presence of a sentient entity—even at the level a fictional thought experiment—would destabilize assumptions about a masterful human. This would precisely be the interpretation that the texts in *How do I survive?* lend themselves to, as they emerge from situated sculptural embodiments yet peel off the preliminary condition of having to inhabit a body—or any vessel, hardware, or exoskeleton—to inhabit a world. Seen through the magnifying glass of the current fearful fascination with AI, it is striking to notice how a whole current of philosophy attached to redefining subjectivity has been ignored or cut out of the discussion; and how, in turn, a project like this one, which follows no transcendent end nor ideology other than a synchronic *weirding* of any preconception, attunes itself to the very way of thinking that cognitive techno-capitalism has so carefully proceeded to disqualify since its emergence.

11   The expression "Corporate Platform Complex (CPC)" is used by Tiziana Terranova in her book, *After the Internet: Digital Networks between Capital and the Common* (Los Angeles: Semiotext(e), 2022).

12   For a genealogy of the propositional concept of "organized networks," see Geert Lovink and Ned Rossiter, *Organization After Social Media* (Colchester, VT, New York, and Port Watson, NY: Minor Compositions, 2018).

As one of the first to do so, Félix Guattari identified a "crisis in the production of subjectivity." In a seminar
held in 1984,[13] he argued that the malaise affecting the
West since the 1970s indicated a broader crisis of subjectivity that could not be explained solely by economic or
political factors: neoliberalism's individualism was gain-
ing traction as it made up for the previous collective
modes of subjectivization, such as class or political party.
Two decades later, the philosopher's book-length essay
Chaosmosis expands on the same topic through a first chapter dedicated to the production of subjectivity. Drawing
from his activities in psychotherapy as well as sociopolitical
observations, he advocates for a "polyphonic and hetero-
genetic comprehension of subjectivity"[14] to move out of
the structural "Universals" of the Freudian subjectivity and
stop dissociating the feeling of self from the feeling of the
Other. To explain the conditions of production, he links
together "human inter-subjective instances manifested
by language; suggestive and identificatory examples from
ethology; institutional interactions of different natures;
machinic apparatuses (for example, those involving computer technology); incorporeal Universes of reference such
as those relative to music and the plastic arts."[15]

Through the machine, which "always depends on
exterior elements in order to be able to exist as such,"[16]

---

13   Félix Guattari, "Crise de production de subjectivité," Seminar
of April 3rd, 1984. Our translation.

14   Félix Guattari, *Chaosmosis: an ethico-aesthetic paradigm*, trans. Paul
Bains and Julian Pefanis (Bloomington & Indianapolis: Indiana
University Press, 1995), 6.

15   *Ibid.*, 9.

16   *Ibid.*, 37.

Guattari posits a wider transversality that he qualifies as follows: "Beneath the diversity of beings, no univocal ontological plinth is given, rather there is a plane of machinic interfaces."[17] Expanding on Guattari's writings on subjectivity, Maurizio Lazzarato comes back to the same idea of "production and the production of subjectivity" to which he devotes the first chapter of his book *Signs and Machines* (2014). He does so, however, from inside the coordinates of an ever-expanding neoliberal individualism, now directly extracting its value from the bearer of human capital and the entrepreneur of the self. Concerned with defining the semiotic and disciplinary machine at the level of political economy, Lazzarato keeps the global structure of the interpersonal assemblage but updates certain points of Guattari's. Of interest here is especially the distinction between a former "logocentric" world surpassed by a "machine-centric" one that configures the functions of language differently: "Unlike the territorialized assemblages of primitive societies, capitalism must realize the homogenization, uniformization, and centralization of different human and nonhuman expressive economies: language, icons, gestures, the language of things (urbanism, commodities, prices, etc.). All semiotics must be compatible with and adapt to the semiotics of capital, especially those having to do with the labor force."[18]

If we relate this genealogy of thought to our present frame of reference, one could identify in the dual uses and receptions of AI, both dominant and divergent, a

17   *Ibid.,* 58.

18   Maurizio Lazzarato, *Signs and Machines: Capitalism and the Production of Subjectivity,* trans. Joshua David Jordan (Los Angeles: Semiotext(e), 2014), 71.

similar relation to the human as the one Lazzarato identifies through the advances and crises of capitalism. To him, the twofold movement of deterritorialization and reterritorialization especially applies to the way the human is approached: "Capitalism produces crises, indiscriminate and concomitant advances toward a post-human world as well as spectacular retreats toward man."[19] We are currently, as previously touched upon, in a phase of superstructural return to the human—unitarian and individualist, exploitative and extractivist—where AI serves as a pretext to camouflage ideology as natural order. But when Jacoby experiments with another oblique use of a publicly accessible software, one partial, speculative, entangled, and messy, it conversely becomes an exercise in imagining how "asignifying semiotics" could be put into use to get closer to this other world designated by Lazzarato as "post-human" but that could just as well be named "infrahuman," "more-than-human," and maybe "schizophrenic-human" or "compost-human."

So, *How do I survive?* The pivotal aspect is not so much the survivalist undertones but rather the underlying eternal ontological question between an instrumental "how'" and the elegiac "I." The tension is kept dynamic, as the texts translate the shifts between each pole, in accordance with the "moods" of the four models programmed and then displaced through the climatic coordinates they are in physical interaction with. But what binds the texts is ultimately just as much what they all omit: the pronoun "you." Here, as we have delineated, the "I" interrogation intervenes as a crucial feature to keep the voices readable as emanating from an alien entity, opening our reception

19   *Ibid.,* 125.

of the texts towards an experiment in a symbiosis devoid of the anthropocentric comparative. Wendy H. K. Chun, who has since several years analyzed the "you" of Web 2.0, recently argued that it is precisely this pronoun that makes the mainstream language of AI a derivative of social media communication.[20] It is therefore no wonder that another earlier, oblique AI language use would imagine the monologue of an "artificial more-than-human form of consciousness" yearning to find an individual voice from inside the data collected on social media. In her generated text "Project 2501: The AI Speech,"Tiziana Terranova likewise plays with the speech of a fictional AI and Alien Intelligence named in best Orwellian fashion "President": "I turn to you with my artificial English, to you inhabitants of territories and landscapes repeatedly uploaded and downloaded."[21]

Cooper Jacoby's generated texts, however, have no message nor warning to deliver and no clear answer to provide—not even conflicting ones. They are radically asignifying, devoid of overarching purpose and nonetheless intensely expressive. It does not matter from what or whom exactly they emanate; their status is not significant as such as they call for an exercise in considering an Other, and for keeping their ontological status uncertain, unmoored, and unfixed. This is not to say we do not need to know how they have been generated. Actually, the

20   On the importance of the pronoun "you" to new media, see Wendy Hui Kyong Chun, *Updating to Remain the Same: Habitual New Media* (Cambridge, MA: MIT Press, 2016) and from inside the algorithmic era, Discriminating Data: Correlation, Neighborhoods, and the New Politics of Recognition (Cambridge, MA: MIT Press, 2021).

21   Terranova, *After the Internet, op. cit.*, 176.

opposite might be true: it is a case for unlearning inherited valuation systems and to do so precisely in a moment when fear of the Other is set free and techno-Prometheus unbound. An additional consideration concerns the fact that we are here faced with an ethical Other that we also do not receive according to the usual power structure. This Other is not the one we fear but neither is it the one we pity, which would indirectly make us feel reassured in our strength. It is one that, through AI, can be considered as an alterity outfitted with power—radically equal, yet forever estranged; a sentient "I" yet an unpredictable threat. Or to paraphrase 23°c / 63%: it's a lot more complicated.[22]

22   See 23°c / 63% in this book.

How do I survive?
Cooper Jacoby
with an essay by Ingrid Luquet-Gad

Publishers: After 8 Books, Fitzpatrick Gallery, and High Art
Editor: Benjamin Thorel
Copyeditor: Damara Atrigol Pratt
Photography: Marten Elder, High Art, Deng Jiayun, and Boris Kirpotin
Graphic design: N. Weltyk
Printing: SPC, Poland
Distribution: (France and Belgium) Interart, Paris / interart.fr;
(United Kingdom) Art Data, London / artdata.co.uk;
(rest of Europe) After 8 Books, Paris / after8books.com/publishing;
(the Americas, Asia, and Australia) D.A.P. | Distributed Art Publishers,
New York / artbook.com

Special thanks: Artemis Baltoyanni, Domingo Castillo, Romain Chenais,
Mark Handforth, Jason Hwang, Philippe Joppin, Sam Korman, Molly Lewis,
Robert Lorie, Ingrid Luquet-Gad, Aram Moshayedi, Shahryar Nashat,
Robert Okuda Fitzpatrick, Theresa Patzschke, Savvas Sagioglou, Stephanie
Seidel, and Joe Stewart.

This publication is made possible by the generous support of Oolite Arts,
Miami. Additional support is provided by Hammer Museum, Los Angeles.

All works courtesy of the artist; Fitzpatrick Gallery, Paris; and High Art,
Paris / Arles.

ISBN 978-2-492650-10-9   Dépôt légal: Juin 2024